Rat

Animal
Series editor: Jonathan Burt

Already published

Crow
Boria Sax

Tortoise
Peter Young

Cockroach
Marion Copeland

Ant
Charlotte Sleigh

Dog
Susan McHugh

Oyster
Rebecca Stott

Bear
Robert E. Bieder

Snake
Drake Stutesman

Forthcoming

Parrot
Paul Carter

Whale
Joe Roman

Falcon
Helen Macdonald

Bee
Claire Preston

Hare
Simon Carnell

Moose
Kevin Jackson

Fly
Steven Connor

Tiger
Susie Green

Fox
Martin Wallen

Crocodile
Richard Freeman

Spider
Katja and Sergiusz Michalski

Duck
Victoria de Rijke

Salmon
Peter Coates

Wolf
Garry Marvin

Rat

Jonathan Burt

REAKTION BOOKS

Published by
REAKTION BOOKS LTD
33 Great Sutton Street
London EC1V ODX, UK
www.reaktionbooks.co.uk

First published 2006
Copyright © Jonathan Burt 2006

Printed and bound in China

British Library Cataloguing in Publication Data

Burt, Jonathan
    Rat. – (Animal)
    1. Rats 2. Animals and civilization
    I. Title
    599.3'52

    ISBN 1 86189 224 1

Contents

Spying on a sorcerer and her rats, a 19th-century illustration.

Introduction

There are so many different roles that the rat plays in human life. When it is an object of admiration it is usually in, say, the show cage at an exhibition, or in a laboratory cage (where it has often been described as a hero/heroine or martyr to science). In the wild, or on the margins of human life, the rat is commonly loathed, the object of vermin control. Either way, one could say that it loses. But the rat fights back. It is not easily containable and its autonomy extends beyond the physical world of the necessities of food and shelter to playing a central, sometimes disturbing, role in human culture. We have a place for it in the classification of the animal kingdom, but its significance goes beyond its ranking and is out of all proportion to its size. The rat is, as some writers have phrased it, a twin of the human, and their mutual history is dark. In fact, the rat has been represented as the very debasement of evolution. If one devolves 'downwards' from the human, one comes not to the ape or monkey but to the rat. By way of introduction to the rat I will explain the shape of this idea.

In 1923 H. P. Lovecraft wrote a horror story entitled 'The Rats in the Walls'. In Lovecraft's comments on it he dwells on the topics of nature and evolution, and discusses the thesis that there were two separate lines of racial development, in his terminology Caucasian and Negro. These derived from different types of ape but at root they shared a common ancestry of extreme bestiality. 'Certain traits in many lower animals suggest, to my mind whose imagination is not dulled by scientific literalism, the beginnings of activities horrible to contemplate in evolved mankind.'[1] 'The Rats in the Walls' is a story, among other things, of such a descent through layers of cultural and natural evolution to the most primeval, base, and horrific level of human activity. What we reach at the bottom of this descent, however, is not the basest of human simian ancestry, but the rat. This play on race, devolution and rats has an echo in T. S. Eliot's near-contemporary anti-Semitic lines 'The rats are underneath the piles. / The jew is underneath the lot.'[2]

Lovecraft's story in brief is this. A man, for various reasons, returns to England from America to repossess and rebuild his ancestral family home. The design of the house itself embodied layers of history, with Gothic features on Romanesque features on Saxon, Roman, Druidic and so on which the narrative peels back as the narrator comes to understand the secret the building conceals. He begins to hear the sounds of rats in the walls, which leads him to investigate the source of the sound. Gathering a team of experts, a huge subterranean cavern under the house is discovered strewn, among other things, with the gnawed remains of countless numbers of skeletons of all different kinds from the most undeveloped human to the most refined. The whole area seems to have been the scene of a primitive rite involving butchery, sacrifice and cannibalism. The narrator then hears the rats coming from the darkest end of the subterranean cavern and in his fear goes mad.[3] The form his madness takes as he begins to fall apart includes speaking in seventeenth-century English, then Middle English, then Latin and Gaelic, finally ending up with a series of primitive sounds. In plunging back through the layers of language he becomes the

This anti-Semitic postcard puns on Maupassant's short story *Boule de Suif* ('Butterball').

most base (in) human being: not ape but rat. In the end he is found crouching over the half-eaten remains of his friend Captain Norrys while being attacked by his cat. The devouring rat does not just stop at corpses or skeletal remains but continues its destruction by disarticulating the psychological joints that hold together the bases of humanity: mind and language.

Why should the rat be such an apt figure for horror and the target of so much hatred and loathing? Clearly this is a question that requires more than the simple answer that they are parasitic little creatures that live in sewers, spread diseases and steal our food. In fact, rats were described as particularly loathsome in various seventeenth- and eighteenth-century texts, mainly on the grounds of their fecundity, long before they were associated with the sewers that appeared as a result of the

ـــــ از نلامت ـــله زرد اوی

ملا

progress of sanitation in the nineteenth century. Although they were seen as harbingers of disease in earlier times, they were not understood to be disease carriers as such until the very end of the nineteenth century, and even the scientific work that proved that fact took a decade or so to be universally accepted. Of course, rats have been seen as thieves throughout history, and in the Middle Ages and the early modern period they were reckoned to be a pest that needed eradicating. However, they were not especially singled out as creatures to be hated or feared. Thus, there remains the question as to why rats have come to have such a low status. Lovecraft points us towards the view that the rat is the agent of human dissolution not only physically but also that it exists in an ambiguous and, in some sense, a dangerous relationship to human thinking and language. It seems to represent evil itself. James Rodwell wrote, in his famous book (1858) on rats, that the word 'rat' sums up its nature. Like an Adamic or magical signature, it contains the essence of what it means in its sound, and is the

The front cover of
James Rodwell's
classic *The Rat*
(London, 1858).

Early observers
didn't distinguish
clearly between
mice and rats: its
nature as absolute
pest is clear from
its actions in steal-
ing the Eucharist;
an illustration
from the *c.* ad
800 *Book of Kells*.

foulest name in British zoology. Harsh and grating to the human ear, Rodwell asks his reader to pronounce it slowly: R–A–T. 'There is such a rattling at the tip of the tongue; and then its sudden and abrupt termination with T reminds us of a bolting horse coming smash against a turnpike gate, and being thereby thrown on its back . . . [the rat is] a kind of devil's lap-dog, that had been kicked out of the infernal regions for being too offensive and too ugly, but which has an everlasting craving for men's hearts and ulcerated toads.'[4]

Because the rat is an object of defilement and because notions of defilement and dirt are very much bound up with key symbolic boundaries of clean and unclean crucial to a general sense of order, then the rat logically should take its place on the far side of a border separating it from clean or the good. But, the symbolic order as much as the physical order is frail and can be easily threatened, especially around dangerous ideas that are so often associated with the horror of the rat: unbounded sexual reproduction, a limitless appetite, and dirt.[5] Cultural attitudes to the rat reveal that it is a pollutant with the ability to move between bodily and symbolic boundaries with an overall trajectory that seems to make it an especially threatening phenomenon as much in the realm of language and thought as in the granary or the food store. Like other dangerous objects, the rat constantly pushes at the edges of the borders set to contain it. Just to make matters worse, it also embodies a certain ambivalence.

The rat is difficult to encode as a straightforwardly loathsome object partly because a refrain common in much writing on rats is that these creatures also inspire a sneaking, if sometimes sullen, admiration. The lascivious, greedy and cannibalistic rat, a stalwart harbourer of a good swatch of the Seven Deadly Sins, is also extremely smart, adaptable and even, for some writers, beautiful. And despite the rat's residence in ditches or sewers, it manages to stay remarkably clean and 'preserves itself from pollution'.

A final reason why the rat so readily invades the psychological preserves of the human lies in the fact that the rat is often understood to be a twin of the human, thriving on those areas of human activity which are themselves deemed to be most problematic, such as war and imperialism. In Hans Zinsser's *Rats, Lice and History*, he characterizes the rat as the shadow of man, following parasitically on the trail of waste and destruction brought by war and imperial conquest. Zinsser's rhetoric ties the rat very closely to the human to the extent that the categories of rat and human constantly cross over each other. Like evil twins with no redemptive qualities, their rapacity, appetites, breeding abilities and adaptability make them world-devouring:

> 'man and the rat are merely, so far, the most successful animals of prey. They are utterly destructive of other forms of life. Neither of them is of the slightest earthly use to any other species of living things . . . Gradually these two have spread across the earth, keeping pace with each other and unable to destroy each other, though continually hostile . . . and, unlike any other species of living things – have made war upon their own kind.'[6]

This idea of human/rat mirroring is very common. A recent writer on rats has said, 'rats live in man's parallel universe, surviving on the effluvia of human society . . . I think of rats as our mirror species, reversed but similar'.[7]

These views of the history of rats and humans suggest two things. First that, unlike the demonic rats in Lovecraft, the rat in this instance does not come from a dark other place but is integral *to*, and, through activities like the harbouring of plague, a

Rats emerging from the pit in a late-19th-century etching for Edgar Allan Poe's story 'The Pit and the Pendulum'.

Alexander Calder's 1948 sculpture *Rat*, a less dark version of the animal.

significant influence *on* human history. The rat cannot be separated from human achievement, yet it also stands as a symptom of human destructiveness. Second, the rat adapts with humans to the ever more complicated structures and networks that are produced by modernization. Networks, such as those of transport and urbanism, are taken advantage of by the rat as it spreads across the world, utilizing large-scale human concentrations of food and shelter. Other networks, on the other hand, are part of the human exploitation of the rat. For example, the breeding networks and genetic (kinship) lineages used by scientists in the creation of laboratory rats, and in the development of genetic engineering. These networks are mirrored by breeders for pet shows and the rat fancy. Thus is the rat in turn exploited. Seen in this context, the labyrinths and puzzle boxes used by behavioural psychologists to understand the mental processes of the rat, and by extension human psychology, seem more than just a straightforward project to improve scientific knowledge. They extend the number of human created networks that the rat ends up having to negotiate, receiving as a reward either food, pain (for instance, the torture of the electric shock), and death. Whether the rat is treated as vermin or hailed as a scientific hero or heroine; in all cases the human intention is always eventually to kill it.

Rather like the divide between scientific martyr and vermin, another boundary the rat crosses over and back again is that which divides the machine from the organic body. The rats that run round mazes in J. B. Watson's behaviourist experiments, published in 1907, are, among other things, helping to understand the notion of efficiency: the squeezing of time and motion. A peculiar version of this can be found in the nineteenth-century rat-pits, where the aim was for the dog to kill a given number of rats within a certain time. Success was measured by speed: a key factor in modern production. H. H. Donaldson, in his 1915 monograph on the rat, comments that the rat is a speeded-up version of the human. The mechanization of labour, and the atomization of its practices on the assembly line, and the acceleration of production thus has a miniature organic counterpart. Furthermore, the breeding of genetically pure and identifiable lines of laboratory rats for endlessly reproducible scientific experiments means that the 'same' body, like a cog in a machine, is being used in different times and places. The rat has become an interchangeable, manipulable, unit. This is exemplified in early twentieth-century experiments in eugenics and the cross-breeding of rats to breed in, or breed out, certain characteristics, such as hair colour.

A particular confluence of networks that took place in the last decade of the nineteenth century and the beginning of the twentieth, pivoted coincidentally, but somehow appropriately, on the Chinese Year of the Rat in 1900. It seems right to dub that period the Time of the Rat because it was then that the impact of the rat on both human history and the pursuit of science was so extensive and influential. All the networks inhabited by the rat, with

Competitive ratting at the Graham Arms public house in London in 1850, from Henry Mayhew's *London Labour and the London Poor*.

the exception of the 'rat fancy' (the breeders of rats for competitive shows), are marked in some way or other by violence, or waste, disease and death. This is not just the verminous underside of the machine age, for it expresses the violence potentially latent in all these networks. In 1894 a rat-borne bubonic plague broke out in Canton and spread to all parts of the world via shipping and railways. Its effects were felt particularly virulently in India, where 10 million people were to die in the twenty years that followed the plague's arrival in Bombay in 1896. Simultaneously in the 1890s, use of the albino rat in laboratory science increased exponentially, and in 1906 the creation of the first breeding lines to standardize albino laboratory rats in Philadelphia at the Wistar Institute was key in the development of animal-based experimentation in large quantities. In the early 1900s there developed a significant use of rats in behavioural psychology, such as in maze learning experiments, and 1901 the first official showing in public

A mid to late 9th-century Thai illustration showing characteristics of the 'Year of the Rat'.

of fancy rats in Britain took place. A little later, in 1909, one of Sigmund Freud's seminal cases, 'The Rat Man', was published. Finally, soldiers' intense exposure to rats on the battlefields of the First World War seems to intensify this impression that the rat, in its own peculiar way, could be described as *a totem animal for modernity*. Furthermore, reflecting the mass production of the consumer age, the rat is both mass object and mass consumer.

Rats spreading across water without human help, from an illuminated missal.

The aim of this book is to provide something like a sketched portrait of the rat in human history and culture. It is not possible to list all the examples of rats in human history, the arts and sciences. There will be consideration of attitudes to rats in cultures other than Western ones, such as those cultures, or groups of people, where the rat is revered, for example in various Asian mythologies. It has to be remembered, however, that reverence and worship also share in structures of pollution and taboo. Such examples act to counterbalance the negative idea of the rat, while at the same time still treating it as a significant and charged object. However, the most historically significant, intense and aggressive preoccupations with the rat are found in the West.

Rat-hunting in the French trenches during the Great War of 1914–18.

The collar of the 'King Rat' of the Grand Order of Water Rats, a charitable society of people in light entertainment.

And yet, even insofar as the rat is an object of hatred, it is not an undifferentiated one. The Satanic rat with its connotations of archaic bestiality is only one strand of a complex of ideas according to which the rat is a dangerous object circulating within various networks and structures, almost like a debased currency, constantly inflating and yet always worthless. The rat is contained within mental and physical systems that are highly structured and organized and yet constantly vulnerable to the rat's ability to gnaw through their foundations. Even if the widespread hatred of the rat seems a straightforward reaction to an apparently loathsome creature, this response does not rest on simple foundations.

1 Natural History

The cultural history of the rat is largely the product of a preoccupation with two particular rats, the black rat (*Rattus rattus*) and the brown rat (*Rattus norvegicus*) – most of this book is focused on them. I use these terms mainly for the sake of convenience, though black rats are not always black nor are brown rats necessarily brown.

To the non-specialist, initial confrontation with the intricacies of rodent classification and evolution can be daunting. The scale of the task is not helped by the fact that rodents make up approximately 40 per cent of the world's mammalian species.[1] That the details of rodent evolution are subject to debate is inevitable given the gaps in the fossil record and the wide variations in dating. Estimates for the divergence of mice (*Mus*) and rats (*Rattus*) from a common creature in the past have ranged from not later than 14 mya (million years ago) to dates in excess of 40 mya.[2] However, it seems in keeping with the omnipresent yet elusive spirit of the rat that it should be part of an order that is so numerous, diverse and difficult to categorize. Rodents are the most speciose mammalian order comprising, according to one account, 1,814 species and 29 families.[3] In recent summary accounts, writers have seen rodents as a remarkable evolutionary success story, because of their extraordinary adaptability to widely different environments, which promises greater attainment than that of humans.

It is intriguing to find scientists commenting that rodents will inherit the earth after humans have died out. This feels like the antithesis to Lovecraft's devolutionary notion that the basest figure is the rat, the bottom of the animal pile as it were. There is a curious mirroring here between human and rat as evolutionary 'successes'. Both species are numerically populous, extremely adaptable to numerous different kinds of environments, and thus, in evolutionary terms, successful in their competition with other species. Furthermore, rats have not suffered to such an extent the environmental destruction that humans have inflicted on many other species. At times they have even benefited from it. As one recent zoology textbook puts it, 'it is quite likely that when human beings decline, at some foreseeable date in the future, the rodents will still be making their way on earth with unabated vigour.'[4] The idea that rodents might inherit the earth shows how far embedded is the idea that they and humans share a common history.

So, where might we find the rat in the vast labyrinthine order of Rodentia? The *Oxford English Dictionary* first notes the occurrence of the word rodent in English writing in the 1830s, and colourfully glosses the order of rodents as the 'gnawers and

Ferdinand Bauer's early 19th-century depiction of the (Australian–New Guinea) water rat, a close relation but not now thought to be a rat proper.

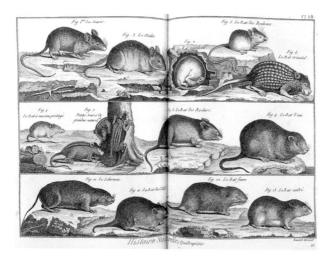

Depictions of rodents from Anselme Desmarest's *Mammalogie, ou description des espèces de mammifères* (1820).

nibblers'. Rodentia derives from the Latin *rodere*, meaning to gnaw. In fact, the classification of rodents has had a changeable history dependent on varying criteria of exactitude and the changing foci of science, the task made difficult, as one naturalist put it in 1876, by 'the immense number and variety of forms which it includes and their puzzling cross-relationships to one another'.[5] In 1819, Blainville divided them into climbers, burrowers and walkers. In 1839, Waterhouse divided them into two groups: rabbits and all the others; he further divided the latter into three groups basing his distinctions on the masseter muscles. In 1855 the German naturalist Brandt labelled Waterhouse's three groups Myomorpha (mouse-like rodents, including rats), Hystricomorpha (porcupine-like rodents), Sciuromorpha (squirrel-like rodents) and these have been something of a basis for subsequent classifications though they have become increasingly complicated. If one follows the standard paths of the classificatory hierarchy of mammals then

The masseter muscle placements have been crucial in the discrimination of different types of rodent: *a.* primitive rodents such as the *Paramys*; *b.* porcupine; *c.* squirrel; *d.* myomorphs such as mice and rats.

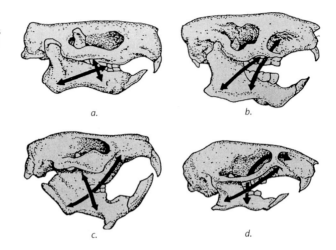

a.

b.

c.

d.

within the myomorphs, *Rattus* is to be found in Murinae in the sub-family of Muridae; a sub-family defined by the distinctive occlusal pattern on the upper cheek-teeth.[6] (Muridae contains some 281 genera and 1326 species, and within that Murinae contains 122 genera and 529 species).[7] For many years natural historians did not distinguish between rats and mice: in the eighteenth century Linnaeus described them collectively as *Mus*. In 1881 French zoologist Trouessart created a sub-category *Epimys* to cover typical rats as distinct from mice, although a German naturalist, Fischer von Waldheim, had already done this in 1803, suggesting the term *Rattus* for the same purpose. Eventually *Epimys* was dropped in favour of *Rattus*.[8]

The story of Rodentia could be summarized by the importance of having good teeth, given that one of the key features of the evolutionary development of the rodent derives from specializations of the incisors and cheek teeth. Rodent incisors are ever-growing with the enamel restricted to the anterior or front part of the tooth. This longitudinal band of hard enamel is

These spirals are the result of unchecked tooth growth in spirals.

backed by a softer dentine which comprises the rest of the tooth, so the tooth wears away differentially keeping the sharp chisel edge. The enamel itself has undergone its own evolution. In some of the earliest fossil rodents, the *Paramyids* from the late Palaeocene (*c.* 60 mya), the enamel is just a strip down the front of the tooth. By the middle of the Eocene (54 to 35 mya), the enamel spreads round the whole front of the tooth.[9] The microstructure of enamel within the tooth shows further remarkable adaptations, producing strong teeth with a structure

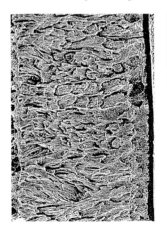 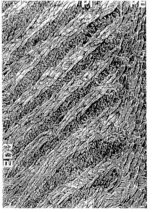

Microscope views of primitive and more developed rodent tooth enamel.

that minimizes the possibilities of cracking. In the teeth of the earliest fossil rodents the enamel is not so defined structurally, is more homogenous and lacks the x-shaped patterning one sees in more recent rodents.[10] In these later creatures the outer layer of the enamel is composed of prisms which are radial, that is running in parallel. The inner portion has prisms patterned according to an x-shape. Under a microscope these can be seen as parallel bands crossed by adjacent bands to create an x-shaped formation.

Other advantageous features of rodents includes their generally small size and a body that is not always highly specialized, with limbs that are very flexible for climbing, running and food gathering. A few modifications to the basic plan of the body such as lengthening the limbs, fusing a few vertebrae, or losing a tail, can produce all manner of different adaptations.[11] Numerous variations in dentition indicate many different kinds of diet and lifestyle. For example, the multi-cusped teeth of mice and squirrels reflect a diet of tubers, berries and seeds, whereas the high prismatic teeth of voles and lemmings are suited to a diet of sedge grass.[12] Rodents also have very fast rates of evolution.[13] In sum, the versatile basic design of rodents gives them not only an ability to occupy many different kinds of environment but accounts also for their longevity as a species.

The details of rodent evolution are much debated, particularly with regard to whether there was a protorodent that evolved from plesiadapids, a type of primitive primate, or whether rodents had a more separate line of evolution.[14] Another possible ancestor are the eurymalids found in Asia and dated to the early Tertiary (*c.* 65 mya), especially *Heomys*, which is the most rodent-like creature from about 60 mya.[15] The important point, however, is that rodents have a very long prehistory. Rodent-like reptiles developed during the Triassic period (230–190 mya) until the late

A conjectural restoration of *Paramys*, an Eocene proto-rat of 55 million years ago.

Jurassic (190–135 mya) when they were replaced by creatures known as multituberculates (meaning 'having many teeth'). These were omnivorous or herbivorous creatures with some similarities to rodents in terms of body size and dentition (they had a pair of lower incisors but without canine teeth). These disappear in the late Eocene. The order Rodentia itself has been around for some 55 million years.[16] The *Paramys* found in North America and Eurasia is one of the earliest of the known rodents from around this time and is described variously by zoologists as like a large squirrel or a mouse-like scampering rodent, some as large as beavers.

The Myomorpha (meaning 'mouse-shaped'), the division that includes the species of rats and mice, were probably descended from an early rat or mouse-like creature known as a scuiravid. Scuiravids are known from deposits in North America and Asia. Myomorphs have different muscles running from the skull to the jaw from other types of rodents, such as squirrels,

A fossil of *Masillamys beegeri*, an Eocene tree-rat, from the Messel shale beds in Germany.

porcupines or beavers. One of the earliest is *Paracricetodon*, found in the early Oligocene deposits (37–24 mya) of Europe. However, it is towards the end of the Miocene epoch that a sudden rise in speciation becomes apparent with the spread of Cricetidae (hamsters and New World mice), then the Microtidae (voles), and the Muridae (rats and mice). Although the fossil record is poor it is reckoned that the murids probably originated in Southeast Asia and it is really in recent times that they have become globally distributed.[17]

Nowadays, apart from the rats that are the main subject of this book, there is a wide variation in the size and behaviour of rats in other families within the Myomorpha, giving a sense of their adaptability. They exist in almost all parts of the world, except the polar regions, and inhabit all manner of environments whether in trees, underground, by water or in human habitations. The stick-nest rat, *Leporillus*, found in Australasia, builds stick nests that can be up to 1.5 m (5 ft) high: when first discovered in 1838 they were thought to be made by Aborigines for signal fires. Some of the largest rats in the world can be found on Flores in Indonesia; these grow up to 46 cm (18 in) long and have a 38-cm (15-in) tail. The Sumatran bamboo rat can reach lengths of 69 cm (27 in) and weigh as much as 4 kg (9 lb). Blind mole rats live underground and can tunnel at a rate of 1 metre every 17 minutes.[18]

The recent evolution of *Rattus* certainly 'mirrors closely the ebb and flow of human endeavours',[19] reflected in the archaeological site maps that depict the locations of early rat remains, clustered in Roman times round trading centres, river networks and coastal sites. Because of the black rat's lower tolerance of cold weather, its spread in non-Mediterranean Europe is completely tied to human movement and settlement. Because they depend on transport networks and a reasonable degree of urbanization, they reveal as much about the history of man as the presence of domestic animals.[20] There are two possible routes by which the black rat travelled west from India: the first

A 'radiation diagram' of the evolution of rats and associated animals.

via the Red Sea, through Alexandria into the Mediterranean and down into Egypt; the second from north-west India to the Persian Gulf and overland into Mesopotamia. One genetic study of modern commensal black rats seems to indicate a radiation beginning with a southern Indian origin, even though the black rat has been described as initially coming from the Indo-Malay region.[21] Because of its resistance to cold weather it is more likely that *Rattus norvegicus* originated in high Central Asia.

So what of the rats themselves? The black rat is smaller than the brown rat. Known sometimes as the ship, roof or even blue rat, it is often a tawny brown to black colour on its dorsal side, and has a paler underbelly which can be lighter brown or slate-coloured. Unlike the brown rat, it is a climber, traditionally associated in buildings with roofs and attics, and will nest in elevated positions like trees. It can breed all the year round, though its preferred time is from March to September. The female can produce between three and five litters a year, with commonly seven to eight young, though this can vary. The gestation period is roughly 23 days, with the young weaned after 3

Rodents from John Hill, *An History of Animals* (London, 1752).

The Rat

The Guinea Pig

The black rat, from Thomas Bell's *A History of British Quadrupeds* (London, 1837).

Black Rat.

The black rat, from William Bingley's *Memoirs of British Quadrupeds* (London, 1809).

to 4 weeks and becoming sexually mature at about 80 days. It is naturally a nocturnal animal. In terms of geographical distribution, as a general rule the nearer one gets to the equator the more black rats and fewer brown rats one finds.[22]

The brown rat, too, has many names: wharf rat, sewer rat, common rat or Norway rat. It is usually dark grey or brown, though it can be white, with a pale grey or greyish brown underbelly. Again, if food and shelter is plentiful, brown rats will breed throughout the year, though winter is often less significant for breeding. Females are receptive for about twenty hours every three to four days. The brown rat is a more grounded animal than the black rat, finding its homes in sewers, under floors, in basements and in all manner of cavities. Gestation is the same as for the black rat, though if the female is still nursing an earlier litter this can take longer. Litters can be as large as fourteen, but generally average between six and eight. Females can be ready to mate as soon as eighteen hours after giving birth and offspring are sexually mature by three months. The bite of the brown rat is extraordinarily powerful and can exert a pressure of up to 7,000 lb per square inch.

John James Audubon's 1843 watercolour of 'The Norway, Brown, or Common House Rat'.

The brown rat, from Thomas Bell's *History of British Quadrupeds* (1837).

Brown or Norway Rat.

The brown rat, from William Bingley's *Memoirs of British Quad-rupeds* (1809).

Evidence of early rats from sites in the Middle East dates to 1600–1550 BC. Even earlier remains, though very rare, have been found in Su Guanu in Italy and in Sardinia (3500 BC), Switzerland and Andalusia in Spain (late Bronze Age), central Italy and Sweden (late Iron Age).[23] However, the Roman period is much better documented for rat remains and includes examples found at Pompei. Rats spread up the Rhine–Rhone river networks in the first and second centuries AD, arriving in Britain where their remains have been found in first- to fourth-century sites in London, Wroxeter and York.[24] It can be inferred from archaeological evidence that the rat populations in Roman times through to the early Middle Ages were more limited than in the period from the eleventh to the fifteenth centuries.

The connection between the black rat and trends in human history is reinforced by evidence that seems to point to an absence of rats during the Dark Ages in Britain, and a general extinction of rats in northern and western Europe. Whilst the rat continued to survive in Italy and the Byzantine east, for instance Greece and Syria, the upheavals in northern Europe and the loss of commercial contact with the Mediterranean ruled out the possibility of reinforcing declining populations of rats, which may also have been affected by phenomena such as climate change and a deterioration in building.[25] There is some evidence that mice (*Mus domesticus*) proved more durable than rats and less vulnerable to shifts in environment and cultural change.[26] With the Vikings and the revival of trade in the ninth century, a return of the rat to Britain appears to have occurred.

The manner of their spread around the world continues to follow this pattern. The black rat arrived on the Pacific coast of South America sometime in the mid-sixteenth century and gained a foothold in Florida in 1565 through the Spanish military garrison at St Augustine. Basque mariners hunting whales took rats northwards to Labrador. The English carried more rats over in the early seventeenth century, and the rats multiplied so fast at the colony of Jamestown in Virginia that they nearly threatened the colony's existence in 1609. The brown rat, *Rattus norvegicus*, was likewise brought to America in the mid-eighteenth century with traders and colonists, and spread inland, arriving in

34

合衆國有名の禽學者某度々の

旅行に少なからぬ多年思慮を殫して撮寫せ

繪本を箱に人親戚に托して置く數月にして

家に帰り箱を開く見ば鼠其内に巣

び畫圖を卷々齧みて碎片となりて

覃茂林に是を見て大に心を傷めり先

數日の間恍惚として失念せる者の如く

既みず人舊商の如く小銃と手に一記簿鉛筆を

勢ひ林に入り一々鳥島を捕へ其形狀を撮寫せしとき三年に

至らずして畫又箱に滿ち撮寫を前時より更に好きを覺ほどを

Rats arrive eventually at the most out-of-the-way places; this stamp from the remote island of Tristan da Cunha commemorates their arrival on the island in 1879.

Kentucky in 1812. Famously, in around 1824 rats ate 200 pictures by the nature artist John James Audubon.[27]

There is an irony in the way that the archaeological picture, in these examples, makes rats a barometer of cultural and commercial strength. Following humans wherever they go, rats seem like a totem figure of human movement and displacement. No matter where they are born, rats always seem to come from somewhere else. The corollary of this is that they are vulnerable to shifts in a combination of environmental and human-influenced conditions. This happened in the Dark Ages and there are modern parallels. For instance, the populations of black rats in Britain, declining since the 1950s, are limited in the main to seaports where, despite their continued arrival on ships, their populations appear to be small and short-lived. This is the result of post-war rebuilding of ports, the use of concrete, the decline of traffic by inland waterways, the transport of goods by container, and people's decreased tolerance of rats.[28]

2 Natural Historians and the Rat

Not only does natural history writing reveal a great deal about how we have come to understand the rat in nature, it also acts as a barometer of the intensification of negative attitudes towards the rat. Although to some extent, increasing knowledge of and increasing dislike of the rat move in parallel, the picture is a complicated one and what constitutes the 'science' of the observation of rats inevitably changes its parameters over time. However, this does not mean that early works describing the rat in the animal kingdom are without interest or insight even if their descriptions of the rat can be remarkably eclectic.

Gessner's *Historiae Animalium*, published from 1551, lists all the different kinds of mice and rats in a long section comprehensibly entitled 'De mure'. Gessner's interest is an encyclopaedic one, and he not only describes their physical characteristics, and tells anecdotes about their behaviour taken from a range of sources, but also gives the different terminologies for mice and rats in different cultures, and comments on their medicinal qualities. He notes the existence of rat kings ('rattorum regem' or 'ratzenkünig'), which he says are bigger than other rats, idle, and fed by their fellows. He also remarks that rats are filled with lust and so depraved that their urine can cause naked flesh to decay.[1] Edward Topsell, who based much of his work on Gessner, brought together a similar set of knowledges in his *Historie of Four-Footed Beasts*, published in 1607.

According to Topsell there are two types of rats, on land and water: *Rattus terrestris* and *Rattus fluviatalis*. Furthermore he saw rats and mice as distinct. The rat was four times the size of the common mouse and had a tail that is long and devoid of hair so that 'it is not unworthily counted venemous, for it seemeth to partake with the nature of Serpents'.[2] The medicinal properties of mice are legion: their bodies should be inserted into wounds and snake bites; water in which a mouse has been 'sod or boyled' is good for 'the inflammation of the iawes or the disease called the Squincie'; and burnt mouse head powder is excellent for cleaning teeth. The dung of rats is useful for curing the falling of hair but it is dangerous when the rat has been raging with lust. Mice and rats are also associated with memory. Bourdon de Sigrais in the eighteenth century claims that

The (relatively) scientific rat, from Conrad Gessner's *Historiae Animalium*.

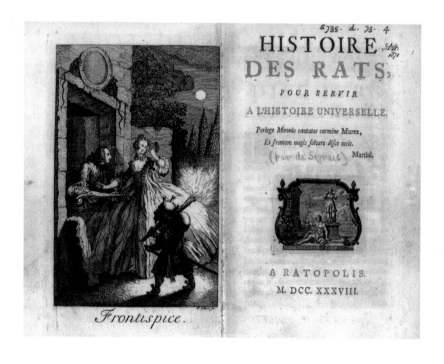

HISTOIRE
DES RATS,
POUR SERVIR
À L'HISTOIRE UNIVERSELLE.

Perlege Mœonio cantatas carmine Mures,
Et frontem nugis solvere disce meis.

(par de Segrais)   Martial.

A RATOPOLIS.
M. DCC. XXXVIII.

Frontispice.

dogs are faithful and cats are fickle because the eating of rats promotes forgetfulness.[3] In the next set of important nature writing on rats, which occurs in the eighteenth century, the rat becomes a much less desirable creature. However, the development of this perspective is not straightforward.

Some writers have claimed that the rat was symbolically refashioned in the nineteenth century as it threatened the new thresholds of cleanliness that accompanied the building of sewers and other sanitary and medical advances. As rats came up out of the sewers they were a visible embodiment of the filth that society was placing out of sight.[4] To some extent this is true; in earlier periods rats were seen primarily as an economic threat, especially

The frontispiece of Bourdon de Sigrais's *Histoire des Rats* (1738), the first book to tell the story from the rats' point of view.

a threat to food in those times when there was not enough for all.[5] However, this picture is more complicated because there are examples of rat hatred in the seventeenth century too. Furthermore, the shift from thief to dirty animal is complicated by the refrain found in many writers that, even when rats inhabit the most foul places, they are remarkably clean animals. In this sense rats are doubly transgressive in the way they cross boundaries of cleanliness and dirt, and also embody those boundaries within themselves. One expression of loathing and disgust towards rats in the seventeenth century has a similarly ambivalent status. Philippus Camerarius writes, 'that although Rattes and Mise be creatures very contemptible, and loathed of all men (as also Plutarch obserueth, That the wise men of Persia slew all that euer they could get of such vermin, because they hated them extreamely, and accounted them abominable before God, as did also the Arabians and Ethiopians) yet God doth vse them for instruments to punish the sinnes that reigne in the world.'[6] Although it is not quite clear how this idea may have impacted on the perception of rats, it seems an interesting coincidence that the rat should come to be despised at the time of the arrival and spread of the brown rat throughout eighteenth-century Europe. As Peter Pallas writes of the brown rat in 1778, it is of all species 'the most foul, the most ferocious, the most pernicious'.[7] However, the more developed hatred and violent language evident in the accounts of rats from eighteenth-century naturalists onwards stems not from dirt but from other forms of transgressive behaviour to do with reproduction and appetite.

In Thomas Bewick's summary description of black and brown rats he closes with the remark, 'the surest way of killing them is by poison'.[8] Similar sentiments are not generally expressed in relation to other creatures. There is no reason to suggest that these sentiments are necessarily out of place in a scientific or philosophical text. However, what makes such remarks interesting where they occur is the virulence with which they are articulated. It may be the case, as I have suggested, that the arrival of the brown rat in the early eighteenth century gave rise to a more considered anti-rat sentiment, though Thomas Pennant in his classification of British quadrupeds is equally scathing towards black rats that gnaw the 'extremities of infants in their sleep' and brown rats which have a dangerous bite and are prepared to turn on humans.[9] Certainly observations of the excesses of rats, whether these are anecdotal or observed, do not help their cause. However, there are examples of a greater sympathy towards the (relatively) indigenous black rat than towards the brown rat.[10]

Charles Waterton, the eccentric Roman Catholic Victorian naturalist, was probably the most famous brown rat hater of the eighteenth century. His father had told the young Charles a fable about the defeat of the black rats by the brown rats told by many Catholics at the time to show how they had come to be exiles in their own land. It was said that brown rats had landed on English soil in 1688 in the boat that brought the Protestant William of Orange over to oust the Catholic James II.[11] Waterton believed that the brown rat came over with the Hanoverians, and he pursued a vigorous and at times bizarre campaign against 'the Hanover rat', as he called it, though he could not stand the idea of cruelty to any other living creature.[12] His team of ratting cats included a wild Malay tiger cat. He was once seen holding a rat by its tail and twirling it through the air, then dashing its brains out while crying out 'Death to the Hanoverians!'[13] In fact, he was gratified on his travels in Italy to note that although 'scarcely anything which has had life in it comes amiss to the Italians in the way of food' the Hanoverian rat was an exception, usually seen dead in the streets and trodden underfoot.[14] His attitude to the black rat was markedly different. He only ever saw one black rat, which he

A watercolour of 1788 by Franz Anton von Schiedel, showing a mole and five rodents, including a lemming, a rat and several mice.

describes as brought to him in a cage and over which he said: 'Poor injured Briton! hard, indeed, has been the fate of thy family! in another generation, at farthest, it will probably sink down into the dust for ever!'[15] Although it was not completely the case that the black rat was disappearing from late eighteenth-century Britain they were becoming less noticeable. Between John Berkenhout's edition of his *Outlines of the Natural History of Great Britain and*

The common rat, the Norway rat and a shrew mouse, from Thomas Pennant's *British Zoology* (1766).

42

Ireland (1769–72) and his *Synopsis* in 1795 he added to the latter's section on the black rat the words 'almost extinct'.[16] Just under a century later James Harting noted that the black rat in Britain was 'so nearly extinct that the occasional capture of a specimen is generally considered worthy of record in some or other of the natural history journals'.[17]

In the later eighteenth century Buffon noted that the rat is one of those creatures that survives by sheer profusion to make up for its small size, and lack of 'arms' or courage. This is the one advantage given by Nature to small animals like these: 'to resist or survive through quantity'.[18] If that system breaks down, however, and there are too many rats and too few resources, they attack each other: the strongest throw themselves on the weakest and 'open up the head and eat first the brains, and then the rest of the body'.[19] The potential for savagery and cannibalism is a key feature of the rat. In Cuvier's classificatory survey of the animal kingdom first published in 1817 there is a similar expression of condemnation within the context of scientific description. Cuvier describes rats as continual eating machines with an extraordinary capacity for destruction disproportionate to their size. This activity takes place in a particular way. The incisors of rodents can scarcely seize a living prey, nor tear the flesh, nor cut foodstuffs. Instead, they file them down, reducing the food by continuous work. This process does not just serve the needs of their bodies for food but also the needs of their teeth, which will grow continuously if broken or unused, to the point of becoming, to use Cuvier's word, 'monstrous'. 'These animals are extremely noxious both due to their fecundity and the voracity with which they gnaw and devour the substances of the whole of nature.'[20] Thus the monstrous is, in effect, the unchecked, and the disproportion of size to scale of destruction is made up for by the continual labour of gnawing. The rat becomes a figure of negative energy and decay, with its teeth constantly nibbling away at the world; a form of negative energy. Its consumption is geared to feeding the animal but also to maintaining the teeth in a particular interdependency between eating and physical form.

Writing at the end of the eighteenth century Thomas Bewick claims that there is no defence against the fecundity of the rat. The only thing that stops their numbers growing to such a size that they would destroy everything is their capacity to kill each other: 'their numbers would soon increase beyond all power of restraint, were it not for an insatiable appetite, that impels them to destroy and devour each other'.[21] Later writers also commented on their boundless sexual appetite (though, in fact, their fecundity is much more limited by natural conditions than is popularly thought). Charles Fothergill noted in 1813 that the rat 'is continually under the furor of love . . . the embraces of the male are admitted immediately after the birth of the vindictive progeny'.[22] Fothergill's vision of the unchecked proliferation of rats is apocalyptic: 'if *rats* were suffered to multiply without . . . restraint . . . not only would fertile plains and rich cities be undermined and destroyed, but the whole surface of the earth in a very few years would be rendered a barren

A woodcut of a 'rat king', an entanglement of live rats perhaps caused by over-crowding, from a 16th-century book of emblems.

'Rat kings' were often thought to be fantasies, but they do occur if rarely – as in this 1914 photograph.

and an hideous waste, covered with myriads of famished *grey rats,* against which man himself would contend in vain'.[23] Fothergill continues in a similarly purple vein when describing their blood lust, cannibalism and terrorizing of females. In 1857, Francis Buckland calculated that the 2,525 rats killed by the famous ratting dog Tiny would, in three years, have turned into '1,633 millions 190,200 living rats'.[24] This statistical game of a limitless expansion of rat populations as if there were no natural restrictions occurs in numerous texts and is part of the construction of their perpetual voracity. One of the most outlandish calculations, by von Fischer in 1872, is to the effect that a single pair of rats could after ten years produce a progeny of 48,319,698,843,030,344,720.[25] Rats manage to bring together the taboo areas of sexual lawlessness and cannibalism. The two are effectively linked. Their appetites are so unrestrained that there is no order: sexual excess goes hand in hand with a cannibalistic barbarism.

These examples suggest that distaste for the rat in the eighteenth and early nineteenth century centres on the notion of appetite and not on notions of dirt; issues of vice rather than hygiene. The rat is loathed because it is overpopulous, brutish and permanently sexualized. This may link up to developing ideas of taste during the seventeenth century which included a greater sensitivity to the drawbacks of surfeit and excess.[26] But there are, as noted above, still traces of ambivalence towards the rat. William Mcgillivray, writing in 1843, reserves particular opprobrium for the brown rat. The brown rat is an audacious animal, audacious enough 'to attack even one of the lords of creation'.[27] However, the black rat is, in some ways, a good creature whose natural instincts are changed by its proximity to man: 'an active, lively, most cleanly, and, I think, beautiful, little quadruped'. Its affectionate concern for its young is unsurpassed by any other animal and if it did not live near man and stuck to woods and pastures it would be delightful. The brown rat, too, is not without some redeeming qualities. Mcgillivray notes its cleanliness and even a certain kind of beauty. Even when it lives 'in the midst of all sorts of filth, it almost invariably preserves itself from pollution; and in parts remote from towns its fur is often possessed of considerable beauty'.[28]

The admirable points of the rat from Mcgillivray's point of view are more manifest when living away from humans. In fact, it is their connection with humans that that corrupts them. A further drawback mentioned by him is that they have no use of any kind to counterbalance their thieving, or make them seem a little less odious. At the same time he cannot help but admire the cunning and sagacity that enables them to survive and defeats all attempts to eradicate them. In many ways, Mcgillivray neatly sums up the complexity of attitudes towards the rat that are still relevant today. The rat is a clean animal living in the middle of filth, a cunning and intelligent creature of no discernible use, a parasite rather than a producer. It is an animal completely locked into human life, yet at the same time taking everything for its own ends. All it feeds is its apparently limitless appetite for anarchy, violence, and a quest for power within its own species. Ultimately the rat treats humans as humans treat other animals. The rat *profits* from the human's own profits, and yet provides no products of any kind. The rat imitates the human's own prodigious appetite and is, like an anti-system, the embodiment of a drive to consume and nothing more.

J. G. Millais, writing at the beginning of the twentieth century and around the time that the theory that rats carry plague was being slowly accepted, offers a more extreme oscillation between the descriptive and the urban horror of rats. The brown rat is 'the best-hated animal in Europe'.[29] It can reach grotesque sizes: he mentions one he killed that was 19 inches (48 cm) long from head

A sympathetic portrayal in *Two Rats* (1884), a work in oils on panel attributed to Vincent van Gogh.

to tail and weighed 2 lb (1 kg). Rats also form the threatening underbelly of the city. 'Underground London seethes at night with a restless sea of rats which do some good by scavenging but are constantly undermining and tunnelling into buildings.'[30] Worse still, they murder the young and the vulnerable, such as tramps and children, in their sleep. In 1904 in Lewisham in London, a six-week-old child was gnawed to death; the left side of the scalp and the upper cheek had been eaten away. Rats have even been known, Millais adds, to eat a pig whilst it is still alive. Perhaps the most horrible of Millais's litany of gothic memories is his description of a bald rat found in an outhouse of his which had a transparent yellow skin 'through which one could see the whole of his entrails working . . . the eyes having no hirsute setting, seemed to be dropping out of his wicked looking head'.[31]

The interconnection between the rat as phobic object and as the object of natural history has its modern counterpart in the fact that most of this kind of research has been done with a view to control and extermination. There were some 3,800 publications worldwide on pest rodents and their control up to 1945. Between 1950 and 1974 this number had increased to 17,000.[32] In the United States during the Second World War, research into

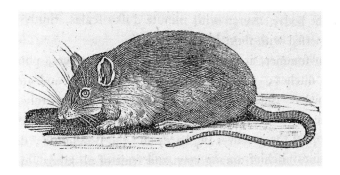

'The Rat', from Thomas Bewick's *History of Quadrupeds* (1800).

rodents centred on the Rodent Ecology Project at Johns Hopkins University, which was a response, first, to the idea that the Germans might use rats to spread disease and, second, to the threat to foodstuffs after the war.[33] A similar project was undertaken in Britain in 1939 arising out of the redirection of the work of the Oxford University's Bureau of Animal Populations on vermin control for the protection of food resources in wartime. This led to the first intensive study in Britain of dietary requirements, habitats and behaviour, as well as the systematic study of poisons and the efficiency of trapping.[34] However, both projects were preceded by studies of rats conducted as part of plague control efforts, especially in India, at the beginning of the century. Thus, the impetus to understand the rat is driven by the desire to control or eradicate it. It is almost as if, in a curious reverse of the idea that rats can foresee disaster and leave a falling house or a sinking ship, humans had already decided that rats were to be singled out as a key enemy before they fully appreciated all the ways in which they were an enemy. The representation of the rat as an object of hatred is linked to the emergence of a detailed knowledge of what they are.

3 Rat Representations

Rats appear throughout history in myths, books, poems, paintings, drawings, films and sculpture, reflecting a long and troubling preoccupation within the human psyche. From a distance, the symbolism of the rat appears to be undifferentiated and chaotic but there are, in fact, common themes and identifiable principles of organization. Rats are fundamentally ambiguous creatures occupying intriguing positions around notions of the sacred, the profane and the apocalyptic. They also have positive characterizations in myths and fables that belie their verminous status. Rats can be elusive and difficult to pin down, revolutionary in some contexts and dangerous and destructive in others. From a cultural point of view the rat is a highly charged figure that can warn and threaten, yet also bring salvation and good fortune.

In the Bible the Hebrew word '*akbar* is given to a wide range of rodents including rats, mice, hamsters and jerboas, with the root meaning of 'corn-eater'.[1] Standard English biblical translations vary as to which rodent is chosen. Although the references are not numerous, they nevertheless reveal these creatures to have a taboo status as well as an association with ideas of multitude and plague. In Leviticus 11.29, those animals 'that teem on the ground' are regarded as unclean and cannot be eaten. Various forms of contact will lead to pollution if when dead they are touched or fall on any article of wood, garment or skin. This

renders the person or materials unclean for the rest of the day. All such teeming creatures are vermin and cannot be eaten (11.41). A more extreme version of the food taboo is found in Isaiah where it is said that anyone eating the flesh of pigs, rats and all vile vermin will die (66.17).

There is one reference in the Old Testament where the presence of rodents coincides with the coming of plague. When the Palestinians capture the Ark of the Covenant from the Israelites and take it to Ashdod, they are visited by a disease of tumours (or haemorrhoids) and a plague of rodents (1 Samuel 6.4ff). As the Palestinians attempt to ward off this scourge they move the Ark to other towns only for the outbreaks to follow them. This episode provides one of the main iconographical bases for associations of rats and plague in art prior to the late nineteenth century and has been taken as an early indication that people understood the links between rodents and plague. For instance, Poussin depicted this though, as one writer notes, the mice show no sign of dying or being sick.[2] However, it is difficult to establish exactly how the association between rodents and plague was understood beyond the presence of animals fore-warning disaster. The passage in Samuel, 'and in the villages and fields in the midst of the country there came forth a multitude of mice; there was the confusion of a great mortality in the city' is an addition in the Latin Vulgate and Greek Septuagint texts and is not in the Hebrew text of the Old Testament nor in English translations such as the King James Bible.[3] The idea of an uncontrollable disease moving from place to place along with the presence of some form of rodent fits with the more general cultural image of rodents as, at the very least, a sign of disease. The ambiguity as to which rodent is actually being referred to may reflect the fact that many varieties of mice and rat were equally damaging and pestilential.

An Egyptian wall painting of the Ramesside period (1295–1069 bc) from Deir al-Medina, near Thebes.

There is another dimension to the plague of Ashod story that has a resonance with later representations of rats: an association with money. When the Palestinians return the Ark to the Israelites, they make a peace offering of five tumours (or haemorrhoids) and five rats made of gold. This puts one in mind of periods of history when the bodies of rats or body parts, usually the tail or the head, were exchanged for money as a form of vermin control. In Britain, for instance, the statutory destruction of vermin begins with birds in 1532–3 but is extended to an increasing list, which includes mammals, from 1566. Towns and villages were responsible for controlling specified birds and animals and payment was made by the church at set rates. Payment on three rats or twelve mice was a penny. These payments continue in the main until the early nineteenth century.[4] Zinsser mentions a story in which Jews in Frankfurt in the fifteenth century had to deliver a 'tax' of 5,000 rats' tails every year.[5] Indeed, as we shall see in many examples in this book from the Chinese horoscope to Freud's Rat Man case, the association of rats with money is an extensive one.

During the periods of the ascendancy of Greece and then Rome, many representations of the rat seem to confirm a strong cultural charge, especially around notions of eating, undoing or unpicking, and that they signal both good and bad fortune. Plenty of superstitions from classical times can be found in later periods in Europe. For instance, when a house is about to fall the rats or mice will leave as fast as they can.[6] Because there is not really a distinction between rats and mice in Greek or Latin, it is difficult to determine precisely which is being referred to.[7] However, Greeks and Romans were well aware that there were many different types of rodents. Aristotle notes different kinds including, for instance, ones in Egypt with bristles like a hedgehog, and others that walk on their two hind legs.[8] Aelian notes

A white and a black rat gnaw at the roots of a tree in a 14th-century Islamic manuscript illustration of the allegorical tale of Balaam and Josaphat.

how, in the area now known as Azerbaijan, during changes of the seasons rats visit the land in hordes and cross rivers by fixing their teeth in one another's tails, making a bodily chain between the banks[9] – a method they also use to pull themselves out of pots into which they have fallen. Both Aelian and Aristotle mention the tremendous damage these rodents can do to crops. As far as fecundity is concerned their reproduction, according to Aristotle, is astonishing when compared to other animals both for the number of young produced and the speed. He cites the example of a female rodent shut in a jar of millet, who was discovered, when released, to have spawned 120 offspring. The most extreme case of rodent fecundity is noted in a district of Persia where a dissected female rat was discovered to have embryos that were themselves pregnant. Some observers noted that rats were so fertile that copulation was unnecessary: they merely had to lick salt to become pregnant, an idea echoed in Plutarch who claimed that rats breed more in ships that carry cargoes of salt.[10] For Pliny, bringing neatly together the twin obsessions with the orality and sexuality of rodents, rats could conceive merely by licking each other.[11]

Aside from ideas of fertility a number of classical stories revolve around Apollo in one of his forms, Apollo Smintheus. *Sminthus* is, for the Trojans and Aeolians, the word for rat or mouse. As with the punishing god of biblical myth, Apollo is both a bringer of plague and a healer. Both Aelian and Strabo tell of the temple of Apollo Smintheus at Chrysa near Hamaxitus, in the Troad, where rats were revered as sacred creatures.[12] They were kept and fed at public expense; white rats had nests under the altar; while a rat stood near the statue of Apollo. Two legends are associated with this. The first is that when tens of thousands of rats ate the crops of the Trojans and Aeolians the oracle at Delphi advised them to sacrifice to Apollo

Smintheus to free them of this plague. The second concerns the founding of the temple. A group of Cretans was told by an oracle that they must settle at the place where the earth-born would make war on them. One night their camp was attacked by rats who ate all the leather of their arms and equipment, 'gnawed through their shield-straps and ate through their bowstrings'. Believing them to be the earth-born of the prophecy they built their temple to Smintheus on the spot. There are a number of similar stories. Herodotus tells how the Egyptians were saved from the army of Sanacherib when a plague of field mice ate through the latter's weapons and they fled. Sethos had gone to the temple shrine of Hephaestus to pray for deliverance and the god had come to him in a dream saying he would send champions. In commemoration a stone statue of Sethos was put in the temple with a rat in his hand and an inscription that said 'look on me, and fear the gods'.[13]

The idea of a god that both brings plague and delivers people echoes the idea of the rat as both curse and saviour and can be found in other parts of the world. The Chams of Indo-China worshipped a rat-god called Yang-tikuh who was sacrificed to when swarms of rats invaded the fields.[14] This ambiguous symbolic power is further reflected in remarks on the superstitions surrounding rats. Pliny notes that they cannot be ignored as portents of future events. They foretold the war with the Marsians (91–88 BC) by gnawing silver shields at Lanuvium, and foretold the death of General Carbo by gnawing the puttees inside his sandals. The appearance of white rats is taken as a joyful omen. There is also an intriguing link with gold; he quotes Theophrastus to the effect that rats steal in gold mines and are caught when their bellies are cut open to reveal their theft.[15]

Superstitions and myths that surround the rat in other parts of the world provide a variety of different outlooks on the rat, not all of them negative.[16] Many involve some form of trickery on the part of the rat and it is noteworthy that in India many of the stories are favourable, whereby the rat is usually helpful or useful.[17] The rat's burrowing and gnawing ability may free someone trapped in a well, for instance, or clear a pathway for humans or other animals. A typical example is the tale of a rat and a camel. When the camel is captured he says he belongs to a rat and is scorned. The rat goes to the king to claim the camel, but he too is dismissed. Then, all the rats gather together at night and gnaw all the saddle girths of the king's horses and cattle to pieces so that he is defeated in battle the next day. The camel escapes with the rat into the jungle.[18] Central to the idea of these animal fables is an undoing of the usual orders of superior and inferior creatures. The rat's size belies its abilities, for instance. But the rat is also the creature, *par excellence*, who undoes the links that keeps the world order together. As Shakespeare writes in *King Lear*, 'such smiling rogues as these,/Like rats, oft bite the holy chords a-twain/Which are t'intrinse t'unloose' (ii.ii.73–5).

Hindus tend to regard the rat as a lucky animal and it is the vehicle of the elephant-headed god Ganesa, who is also known as Akhuratha – 'rat-borne'.[19] Ganesa is the god of obstacles *and* the overcoming of obstacles as well as a god to be remembered when journeys are undertaken.[20] The designation of rat in Sanskrit is *musaka*, derived from *mus* meaning 'stealing', 'removing' or 'destroying'. The synonym for rat (*akhu*) means, among other things, thief. For some writers this means that the rat at the foot of Ganesa expresses the overcoming of destruction. The early twentieth-century temple dedicated to the fifteenth-century female mystic Karni Mata, near the Indian city of Bikaner, holds rats to be the incarnation of human beings and thus sacred. Thousands of rats live in the temple where they are fed

The Hindu god
Vinayak (Ganesa)
with his emblem-
atic rat assistant
'vehicles'
(*vahanas*), in a
stone carving from
Nepal.

A metal plaque
showing the
Hindu goddess
Bhagwati Karniji
(Karni Mata) with
her attendant rats.

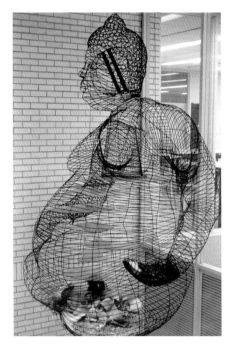

Remo Campo-piano, *Rat-Buddha*, a mixed-media installation (including live rats) at the Minneapolis College of Art and Design, 1989.

opposite
Rats incorporated into the structure of the temple of Karni Mata at Deshnoke, near Bikaner, Rajasthan, built in the early 1900s.

A 1920s magazine illustration of the feeding of the sacred rats at the temple of Karni Mata in Rajasthan.

The sacred rats at the temple of Karni Mata today.

and protected. One legend holds that Karni Mata failed to revive the dead child of a storyteller and subsequently vowed never to allow anyone to fall into the hands of the god of death. Thus the dead temporarily inhabit the bodies of rats before being reborn. The reverence for rats in a land that has been so ravaged by rat-borne plague reveals again the remarkable capacity of rats to occupy many different symbolic roles.

The rat is a key figure in the Chinese horoscope and there are a number of different versions of the myth explaining how the horoscope was divided up. Common to them all is that the animals were invited to meet Buddha or, in other versions, the Jade Emperor. The Jade Emperor had no time to visit the earth

This Japanese warrior in fact has the spirit of a rat, as his shadow reveals; a Robin Hood-like figure whose nickname was 'Rat Boy', in a wood-block print by Utagawa Toyokami, c. 1840.

and wished to see what the animals looked like. As a reward for their appearance the calendar was duly divided up amongst them. The characteristics of people born under the sign of the Rat include charm and imagination. More significantly it is a sign of business. There is a parallel to this in Japanese mythology. The Daikoku, a patron deity of members of the financial profession, as well as artisans and farmers, is one of the Seven Lucky Gods of Japan. He is important for things like crop growth and it is significant that the animal he is associated with is the rat. Although it may seem contradictory that the god of plenty should be associated with the parasitical rat, the idea is that, 'with surplus grain comes the inevitable freeloader who, however, is viewed as non-threatening in a context of overflowing abundance'.[21]

In the West, the fable collections of Aesop and La Fontaine place the rat in a more overtly moralizing and didactic framework; editions are frequently accompanied by moral commentary. However, the valuation of self-interest provides a seam of irony that runs throughout the fable tradition. Reversals of role which celebrate the fact that great and the small need each other are frequently undermined: the mouse who is granted the hand of a lion king's daughter because he has rescued the lion when tied in a net, is accidentally stepped on by the bride-to-be. One of the main features of the rat in Western fables is its long-standing enmity with frogs. The most elaborate tale of their conflict, mentioned in Plutarch, is the *Batrachomyomachia*, a tale that climaxes in a giant battle in which the frogs are saved from defeat by the last minute arrival of the crayfish. This story has a long literary tradition in print, existing in at least 162 editions in many languages from 1474.[22] The intelligence of the rat is also key to its role in fables, prompting La Fontaine to the longest, and most serious, philosophical meditation in all of his fables, on the difference between the minds of animals and humans at the end of 'Les deux rats, le renard et l'oeuf'.[23] As Roger L'Estrange writes, we ought to be instructed by the example of the 'wit of vermine' not to make the same mistake twice but 'in despite of claps and surfeits, men we see will be fuddling on and whoring still'.[24]

There is a group of Indian myths in which rats are linked to sex. The gnawing ability of the rat is the key to a number of myths on the origins of sexual intercourse and sexual parts. According to the Jhorias, in the days when women had no sexual organs it was the rat who made the first opening. There is a similar myth amongst the Hill Saora concerning the origin of the male rectum, according to which a rat was put in a man's belly and burrowed its way out through his backside.[25] Another

An anonymous 17th-century Italian *Batrachomyomachia*, a 'battle between the frogs and the mice' that has its origins in Classical literature.

Rats with eggs, a favoured food, in an 18th-century illustration to an earlier fable by Jean de La Fontaine.

Rats and eggs on a fan decorated by the 17th-century Japanese artist Satake Eikai.

myth refers to a time when women had no vagina and conception took place through their navels. One day a man named Birkati Mussi had a rat that bit between his wife's legs and blood came out; when the man saw the new cavity he entered it just as the blood was flowing out and his eyes burst open; the rat brought medicine so that the man could see again. 'But since then we never approach our wives during their periods, and we never eat this rat – it stinks, for it is covered with old blood.'[26] Another myth narrates how a man with a penis a cubit long kills his wives during lovemaking 'as a result of his terrible penis'. One woman, however, decides that she will not suffer the same fate so she knocks him out with alcohol and cuts his penis down to a manageable size. The rest she throws on the ground from where it jumps up and runs into a hole: 'this was the first rat and it was as dirty as the thing it came from'.[27]

The equation of the rat with sexual parts is an obvious symptom of the rat's abject status. In Classical Greece Aelian quotes from Epicrates to the effect that a woman who is referred to as 'an absolute mousehole' is a woman lecherous beyond measure.[28] Similar sentiments are found in sixteenth-century Europe where the vagina is described as a trap or mousehole for the phallic rat or mouse. A seventeenth-century variant sees cats as female sexual parts and rats as penises.[29] The sexual connotations of the rat can take other forms, however. It was rumoured that Marcel Proust had a fetish for being sexually stimulated by stabbing rats with pins or seeing famished rats fighting each other.[30] Rats were also often sexualized when associated with witches as their familiars. In the trial of Margaret and Philippa Flower, executed at Lincoln in 1618, it was said that the Devil came to them in forms such as a cat, rat or dog. Philippa confessed that a white rat had sucked at her left breast for three or four years and Margaret that 'she had

two familiar spirits sucking on her, the one white, the other black-spotted within the inward parts of her secrets'.[31]

In other parts of the world there is a similar ambivalence toward the rat. In Hawaii, where rat shooting was a favourite betting sport among chiefs, the rat figures prominently in stories of the *kupua* – supernatural beings with shapeshifting abilities. In one story Makali'i, a mythical ruler, stores up food and in times of famine puts it out of reach in a net. The rats travel over the earth in search of food and find nothing but then, looking up to heaven, they see the net. One rat climbs onto the net via the clouds and a rainbow, nibbles the ropes of the net and the food falls, restocking the earth.[32] In a Tongan myth, similar to western fables of rats being helped across streams or stuck in sinking boats, an octopus helps a rat off a sinking boat. As the octopus swims the rat defecates and urinates on its head and, as it hops onto the shore, cries out 'Octopus, feel your head'. The octopus became the sworn enemy of the rat. When Tongans try to catch octopus they make a crude resemblance of a rat with a stone, two large cowrie shells and a twig, which they dangle in the water. This is called a *makafeke*, or octopus stone.[33] Again, the rat is not simply a figure associated with water but one that crosses

This carving from a Maori meeting house in Auckland, New Zealand, shows Ruanui, the captain of an early colonizing canoe, with a *kiore* rat on his shoulder. Rats were carried on the canoes as food sources, and genetic analysis of their remains has helped trace the human settlement of Oceania.

boundaries, polluting or causing problems as it does so. In the West rats are associated with bad luck in relation to fishing and boats. In Banff in Scotland it was recorded in 1886 that the word 'rat' was never to be uttered when the lines were being baited.[34]

Superstitions noted by British folklorists about the rat reflect most of the themes mentioned above. On the negative side it

A 1950s enact-
ment, in Hamelin,
Germany, of the
Pied Piper story.

was seen as bad luck if rats gnawed at your clothes; gnawing the
hangings in a room was reckoned to forewarn of a death in the
family. However, neighbouring communities could have quite
opposite attitudes to rats, as in Aberdeen in Scotland. One local
community saw the rat as bringing bad luck, whereas the other
saw rats as lucky and their arrival in the house to be a harbinger
of money.[35] In parallel with the idea that rats always seem to
appear mysteriously from somewhere else (the Orient, underground passages), in folklore the movements of the rat do not
obey the normal rules by which creatures circulate in the physical world. In a letter written to the journal *Folk-lore* in 1955, an
itinerant man was described who visited farms to get rid of rats.
He played a whistle, like the Pied Piper, and placed in the rat
holes some written incantations. Then the rats would assemble
in a body and disappear, although it was not known where they
went; certainly not to neighbouring farms.[36] The idea that the
disappearance of rodents can be as unpredictable as their
appearance has a long tradition. Pliny notes how the appearance of field mice is always surprising but no less so than their
disappearance. 'It is a puzzle how such a multitude can be so

suddenly destroyed for they are never found dead, nor has anyone ever dug up a dead mouse in a field in winter.'[37] Power over rats can be as dark as the power of rats to plague and disrupt human life. In a curious little book published in 1905, Sylvanus Thompson records a number of different versions of the Pied Piper story. One has three pipers piping away three plagues – ants, mice and rats. Another has a Capuchin friar in 1240 using magic, a book and a demon to lure rats into the river. When the farmers refuse his promised reward he lures away their livestock.[38] Many of the ideas in the Pied Piper legend lock into ideas both about plague and money. In the Robert Browning version the non-payment of a reward to the Piper leads to the piping away of the children. The charmer of rats is himself a marginal devil-like figure, 'a degraded Orpheus'.[39]

At the other end of the spectrum is the holy figure of St Gertrude, who lived in Nivelles between 631 and 659. From the mid-fifteenth century in different parts of Europe (Alsace,

St Gertrude, the patron saint of rats, reading and praying, from the 15th-century *Book of Hours of the Duke of Savoy*.

A cat preaching to rats in a capital letter from an early 11th-century English manuscript.

Catalonia and Austria) she became associated with rats and mice. In keeping with the presence of rats in other religious contexts both Christian and non-Christian, the iconography in illuminated manuscripts and book illustrations from the late Middle Ages onwards, in which rats crawl over St Gertrude while she sits, juxtaposes sanctity with defilement. As the twelfth-century Cistercian St Bernard of Clairvaux wrote, 'the impurity of unclean desires . . . are like rats gnawing the posteriors'.[40] There are a number of ways of reading the imagery of St Gertrude, the most obvious is that she is attracting the evil of the rats towards her in order to master it. But there are all manner of resonances which the figure of the rat opens up here, not the least of which are ambiguities at the heart of Christian holiness. In his study of medieval myths, for instance, Sabine

Baring-Gould cites an 1843 German volume entitled *Die Attribute der Heiligen*, whereby St Gertrude is presented as the patroness of fleeting souls. For Baring-Gould, this is a pagan trait because St Gertrude occupies the place of the ancient Teutonic goddess Holda or Perchta, the receiver of souls of maidens and children.[41] Baring Gould explains that in Teutonic and Scandinavian beliefs rats and mice were seen as souls of the dead, which is why rats deserting a falling house can be seen as a reference to the soul leaving a crumbling body.[42] The rat exists in other forms of Christian iconography; rats appear on carved globes found in some fifteenth-century French churches.[43]

There are more extreme stories of the rat as a divine agent. The well-known story of Bishop Hatto, who hoarded grain during times of famine and burnt starving people in a barn is a case in point. He was pursued and eaten by rats.[44] There are a number of other legends of bishops eaten by rats including Bishop Wilderof of Strasburg in 997, for having suppressed a convent. Another subject of fascination in the sixteenth century was King Poppiel, who poisoned his relatives at a feast to secure his position on the throne: rats arose from the corpses of his uncles and ate the tyrant as well as his wife and children. Baring Gould suggests that some of these tales have their origins in propitiatory

Rats on a misericord in a church in Champeaux, France.

Rats on a capital in the 14th-century chapel of the Virgin in Coutances Cathedral, France.

In this 16th-century woodcut, the grain-hoarding Bishop Hatto of Mainz is pursued by rats.

John La Farge's 1880s wood engraving of the Bishop Hatto story.

PARLIAMENTARY-REFORM,—or—Opposition-Rats, leaving the House they had Undermined.

human sacrifices made in 'heathen' times of famine. The rat is understood to be a link between a pagan and Christian past. It embodies a type of sympathetic magic in the fact that the rat is the most appropriate creature to punish greed and avarice. It is the excessive requirements of the greedy human appetite, the surplus stores of foodstuffs, that produce the multitudes of rats in the first place. Modern writers such as James Joyce, Samuel Beckett and Thomas Pynchon have played on this ambiguity around rats and religious belief, using them as images that undermine or parody the hierarchies of Christian thinking.[45]

William Neason, ratcatcher, at work in the London sewers, *c.* 1850, from Henry Mayhew's *London Labour and the London Poor.*

Baring Gould's association of rats with primitive beliefs has a modern counterpart in Christopher Herbert's interpretation of the role of rats in Henry Mayhew's *London Labour and the London Poor* (1851), though here it is given a more sociological context. Mayhew is particularly interested in the role of rats in the city with regard to rat catchers, sewermen, and the sport of killing rats in pits. For Herbert, the killing of rats is a 'ceremony of *sacrifice*. This is moreover a sacrifice of a special kind: that of a notoriously filthy animal that stands in the place of a tribal totem, the kindred spirit (in Mayhew's imagination, at any rate)

The celebrated bull terrier Billy killing 100 rats in under 12 minutes at the Westminster pit, 13 May 1821.

of the "nomadic horde" of the poor.'[46] There are a number of strands that make up this idea. The linking of physical and moral dirt appears in both the figure of the rat and Mayhew's characterization of impoverished people. Rats symbolize, par excellence, the correlation of sexual lust and filth and thus form a 'quintessential image of the bodily drives that "Hebraic" Victorian culture (as Matthew Arnold called it) defines as dirty and strives to suppress'.[47] Furthermore, that which is most reviled is also a subject of fascination, reflecting Victorian culture's ambivalent obsession with its own underworld.[48]

In the twentieth century the dark connections between rats and humans are foregrounded around apocalyptic themes and influenced to a great extent by the rat's central importance in science. In a novel by Hugh Sykes Davis, *The Papers of Andrew Melmoth*, Melmoth, a scientist who works on rats, eventually disappears into the sewers, apparently to live among them, having become convinced that rats are capable of some sort of sign

language. Haunted by the possibility of nuclear annihilation Sykes Davis comments that rats 'may be at the beginning of all that will survive of any organisation on this planet'.[49] The rat is figured as a creature free from affection, duty, conscience, disgust and, importantly, kindness and cruelty. The sole mainspring of its social organization is a single-minded force and cunning.[50] However, the human drive towards the nuclear apocalypse can equally be seen as singleminded, involving actions beyond affection and conscience and pathologically motivated by a power-driven and suicidal self-interest. At the apocalypse human and rat swap identities. In Günter Grass's novel, *The Rat*, the figure known as the She Rat lectures the narrator on the planet humans have destroyed as he, the last survivor, orbits the earth and the rats repopulate the planet as its new heirs.

Rat painting by
Manon Cleary.

The rat from its position as victim in science becomes in fiction a more positive figure. It represents a strange warning to humans recommending that they behave less like rats to avoid annihilation. This also implies a deep *unreason* at the heart of the rat/human connection, which parallels the destructive potential and violence inherent in certain aspects of science. In a sense, this has long been recognized. As Bourdon de Sigrais noted in the eighteenth century, the expression 'to have the rats' ('avoir des rats') is a sign of madness and yet, at the same time, the history of rats is inextricably connected to human nature: 'learned people who have examined the nature and character of rats have found in them our inclinations, passions, vices and virtues'.[51] De Sigrais would have probably been astounded by the extremes this combination of madness and identification would reach in the twentieth century. In William Kotzwinkle's satire on laboratory science *Dr Rat*, the narrator is a rat driven mad by the experiments to which he has been subject. He catalogues some horrific examples, such as one in which eggs are removed from a female rat's body and are then grafted on to different parts of a male rat's body, including its eyeballs. However he upholds the principles of scientific experimentation and fights to uphold the standards of human science in the face of a revolution that takes place amongst the laboratory animals. In his defence of the laboratory he ends up bombarding the rebels with bottles containing chemical warfare materials and finally, appropriately enough, ends up hurling a bottle containing bubonic plague. Other novels which, though different in tone, play on similar themes include Robert C. O'Brien's *The Secret of the NIMH* and Constantine Fitzgibbon's *The Rat Report*. In the latter, which also predicts an apocalypse in which humans and rats will fight each other for survival, it is the policy of the rats to keep humans reasonably docile and in adequate numbers to feed the rat species, though they occasionally need to be kept in check by 'periodic and selective wars and plagues'.[52]

In two canonical novels of the mid-twentieth century, *The Plague* (1947) by Albert Camus and *1984* (1949) by George Orwell, rats play a key role. In both, though in different ways, rats threaten the human order physically, culturally and psychologically. In *1984* the significance of the rat is more peripheral yet its presence seems somehow appropriate as Winston Smith, the central character, makes his hopeless stand against the dissolution, or rather restructuring, of language, history and thought into a monolithic expression of Party ideology. Smith's two objects of hatred, rats and the Party, parallel each other in their barbarism. His recurrent nightmare is of facing a wall behind which something unspeakable threatens, implied to be

A prefiguration of the torture scene in Orwell's *1984* in a detail from Hieronymus Bosch's *Garden of Earthly Delights* (*c.* 1510).

a rat, and yet also all manner of forms of madness, as represented by the Party including its doublethink – 'the power of holding two contradictory beliefs in one's mind simultaneously, and accepting both of them'.[53] The final breaking of Winston Smith under torture is when a cage containing two hungry rats is to be strapped to his face. As his torturer says, 'they will leap onto your face and bore straight into it. Sometimes they attack the eyes first. Sometimes they burrow through the cheeks and devour the tongue . . . It was a common punishment in Imperial China.'[54] In a novel in which faces play such a significant part, the face of Big Brother and that of the main enemy of the State, Emmanuel Goldstein, Smith had learned to control his own, to give nothing away about his inner thoughts. With the threat of the rats he succumbs: if the rats have not pierced his face, the Party has effectively succeeded in penetrating it and has undone his thought processes. Orwell had a lifelong obsession with rats and in the Spanish Civil War was more worried about the rats in the trenches than the bullets. As he once wrote, 'if there is one thing I hate more than another it is a rat running over me in the darkness'.[55] In Camus' *The Plague*, rat-borne disease

79

isolates the town of Oran. Isolated correspondence with the outside world becomes increasingly mechanical. 'Week after week we were reduced to starting the same letter over again and copying out the same appeals, so that after a time words which had at first been torn bleeding from our hearts became void of sense.'[56] The dying rats presage not just plague but the emptying of language.

The treatment of rats in poetry also changes over time. Of course generalization is difficult over many different types of poem, from the comic and entertaining, such as children's poetry and rhymed fables, to more serious forms from all round the world. A moral discourse involving rats can be found in poetic fables. In rare instances, things to be remembered about rats may have direct practical implications. Thomas Tusser's *Five Hundred Pointes of Good Husbandrie* (1580), for instance, recommends 'Take heede how thou laiest, the bane for rats/for poisoning servant, thy selfe and thy brats.' However, although rats are often seen as low creatures, their loathsome qualities become more prevalent in the nineteenth and especially the twentieth centuries. In serious verse their physical repugnance comes to the fore. There are fewer examples of positive or even ambivalent readings of the rat in recent poetry where rats are often treated purely in terms of bodily disgust. For example, as Seamus Heaney writes in 'An Advancement of Learning', 'a rat/Slimed out of the water and/My throat sickened so quickly . . . This terror, cold, wet-furred, small clawed/Retreated up a pipe for sewage.'[57]

Numerous earlier verse fables involve stealing food, outwitting, or as often as not, failing to outwit, cats and other enemies. John Gay's fable 'The Rat-Catcher and the Rats', which turns on a competition between the cat and the rat-catcher as to who is going to monopolize the pursuit of vermin, begins with a wonderfully opulent account of food as the rats raid the kitchen every night.

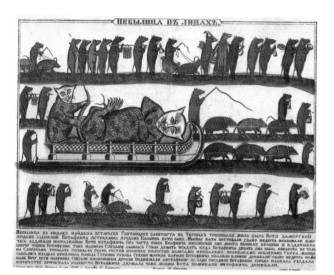

Rats catch a cat, as the world is turned upside-down in an 1850s Russian 'lubok' woodcut print.

They undermin'd whole sides of bacon,
Her cheese was sapped, her tarts were taken,
Her pastys, fenc'd with thickest paste,
Were all demolish'd and laid waste.

Fighting with the cat over the business of protecting such sensual provisions causes the rat-catcher to remark that, without cats, 'we rat-catchers might raise our fees,/ Sole guardians of a nation's cheese!' In most fables and early humourous poems about rats, eating and the conflict around appetite is inevitably central. There is another strand to these tales, where rats turn their appetite onto language itself. In a humorous ballad written in 1736, 'The Rape of the Trap', a rat eats the books in a scholar's room. 'This rat would devour/More sense in an hour,/Than I could write – in twenty.' As the rat lays waste to his library the scholar becomes bereft: 'With grief my Muse rehearses;/How freely he would dine/On some bulky school divine,/And for desert – eat verses.' The ingestion of all this learning causes the rat to outwit the scholar: he lays a trap which the rat simply drags away. In Richard Braithwait's 'In Phyloetum' (in *A Strappado for the Divell*, 1615), the rat eats a love poem when the Phyloetus poet falls asleep and the rat comes to embody the poem:

> If I were to be Judge as such may be,
> The Rat should be in love, Phyloetus free,
> That seeing th' saucy Rat to love enthrall'd,
> Love-bayne hereafter might be rats-Baine call'd.

In the eating of books and words in these fables and ballads the rat maintains its status as pest but not as object of disgust.

By contrast in the Heaney poem quoted briefly above, the rat slobbers and smudges the silence. It slimes out of the water causing the poet to sicken and sweat. For Ted Hughes, in 'Rat Psalm', the poetic phonetic rat borders on the edge of absurdity: the 'riff-raff of the roof space'; 'the Rat, the Rat, the Ratatat/The house's poltergeist, shaped like a shuttle' and, finally, as the poem dissolves into nonsense, 'cupboard adder', 'sprinty-dinty', 'pintle-bum'.[58] For Hughes the rat is also a scapegoat, 'the Little Jesus in the wilderness/Carrying the sins of the house/Into every dish, the hated one.' In Alan Sillitoe's long poem 'The Rats', the rats who stand for various aspects of officialdom and social control

> speak corruption . . .
> The heart stops breeding fields of verity
> Becomes an eggtimer overworked and spun
> By propaganda whose ignoble run
> Of words begets not progress but obesity.[59]

'Rat- machinations roped with force/Imprison beauty in a cage/Encircle it with propaganda morse.' These poetic rats, ignoble and disgusting, make some sort of sense at the limits of language but, like the mystifications of Sillitoe's 'propaganda morse' code, you can never really get a fix on what you hear: the rat heard or half-seen is like a language only half-understood.

Because rats are understood as one of the consequences of the effects of war, feeding off chaos and disorder, one might expect this to be especially reflected in war poetry. Wartime memoirs and eye-witness accounts of rats are commonplace, especially from the period of the First World War to the Vietnam war.[60] Rats were particularly hated in the First World War. As one soldier wrote, 'during the period I had been in the trenches in 1915, there had been an enormous number of rats which ran along the top of the trenches, or swam, snout above the water, through the sodden front and support lines. These rats could be the size of small cats, for there were any number of dead bodies near the lines on which to feed.'[61] Sometimes there would be rat-killing parties where they were smoked out of their holes with cordite and clubbed to death. Soldiers and rats became interchangeable as humans shared with rats the underside of civilization. In David Jones's *In Parenthesis*,

> you can hear the rat of no-man's land
> rut out intricacies,
> weasel out his patient workings,
> scrut, scrut sscrut . . .
> You can hear his carrying-parties rustle with our
>   corruptions . . .
> at night feast on the broken of us.[62]

These creatures embody human degradation, carrying out the same practices in no man's land as their human counterparts with their excavations and their stripping of the dead. Yet they take no sides and in that sense capture a more general spirit of war. In perhaps the most famous lines about a rat in a First World War poem, from Isaac Rosenberg's 'Break of Day in the Trenches', the droll rat with 'cosmopolitan sympathies' moves as it pleases:

> now you have touched this English hand
> You will do the same to a German –
> Soon, no doubt, if it be your pleasure
> To cross the sleeping green between.[63]

Rosenberg attributes to this 'queer sardonic rat' a sense of superiority as it passes between the armies, grinning inwardly. Despite its low status as vermin, *in extremis* the rat is a more effective creature. The rat does not invert the hierarchy of creatures with humans at the top of the pile now at the bottom: the war has already done that.

'That Horrid Rat Again', bullying humans in an 1890s stereoscope photograph.

Rats in film tend to occupy predictable positions as objects of horror or in association with low life. The rat lends itself to horror films either attacking humans or figuring as a totemic symbol of evil, for example, Christophe Ali and Nicolas Bolinauri's *Le Rat* (2001) about a killer; Bruno Mattei's *Notte di Terrore* (1984) in which, after a strange genetic mutation, mankind starts turning into a race with the heads of rats; *The Rats* (2002) where genetically modified rats overrun Manhattan; and so on. The Spanish film *Las Ratas* (1997), directed by Antonio Giménez-Rico, tells of a man and his son who live on the outskirts of a village in a cave and catch water-rats to sell for food, equating rats with the marginalized poor. Morally dubious characters such as the black marketeer in a Japanese prisoner of war camp in *King Rat* (1965), who sells cooked rat to officers under the pretence that it is 'jungle deer', are commonplace. One of the few films with human-rat relations central to the plot is *Willard*, first made in 1971, remade with some differences in 2003. A young man uses his power over a group of rats to destroy his bullying boss but in the end they destroy him.

Although in general film does not reveal the most subtle version of the many cultural manifestations of the rat, technical problems presented by the filming of rats illustrate their status as problematic creatures. The early filmmaker Alice Blaché had used rats in a number of films in 1913 but, during the filming of *The Pit and the Pendulum* (1913), lost control of them completely. An actor was tied to a torture rack with ropes smeared with food and the rats let loose for the shot. They promptly moved on from the ropes to the actor himself. The film crew then attempted to destroy the rats; they 'tossed into their midst an enormous cat, who, horrified, jumped the barrier at one bound'. Equally unsuccessful efforts were made with a bulldog and finally the film cast and crew had to finish the rats off with clubs and cudgels.[64]

Animatronic rats in Glen Morgan's 1993 film *Willard*.

Rehearsing special effects for *Willard*, from Julie Ng's 1993 making-of documentary *The Year of the Rat*.

During the filming of *Nosferatu – Phantom of the Night* (1979), director Werner Herzog fell into dispute with the authorities in Delft, where he was filming, over his attempt to bring in thousands of rats from Hungary for a sequence in one of the town squares. By the time thirteen thousand rats were established in a barn in overcrowded cages, having not been given food or water for three days, they were engaged in a vicious cannibalism. 'In every cage you could see a great devouring, perhaps ten dead or partly eaten rats and a hundred or more of their companions who were gorging themselves, starting with the belly and moving on to the muscle mass, leaving in the end nothing but the tips of tails and a few stray incisors.'[65] Eventually the surviving rats were dyed grey (some died in this process too) and blow-dried to save them from pneumonia. During the filming, no one in the cast was willing to put their bare foot into a coffin full of rats for one of the takes. Eventually Herzog did it himself.[66] Between the first and second making of *Willard* the advent of animatronics and CGI had changed the possibilities of filming with animals. In the first filming of *Willard* live rats were thrown across the camera when they wanted shots of rats jumping. In the second version a combination of live and animatronic rats were used, with some five hundred live rats as background extras. The two main rat characters of the film were provided

by a number of Gambian pouched rats, large rats weighing some 3 kg (7 lb), each trained to do a specific action.[67]

This brief survey of the representation of rats globally and historically reveals some intriguing recurrent themes. Rats are ambivalent creatures, they move between good and bad categories exhibiting qualities such as cunning and the ability to survive while also being seen as thieves and harbourers of disease. They are revered and despised. They have a longstanding status as harbingers of plague and disaster, which is reworked in twentieth-century fictions of the apocalypse. They have also been increasingly the object of physical disgust and virulent hatred as we approach the present day, especially in the last three hundred

David Falconer's sculpture, *Vermin Death Star,* 2000–02, composed of thousands of cast-metal rats.

years. Their destructiveness is also seen as a threat to forms of
order such as language and reason. Their significance in human
culture appears to be out of all proportion to their physical size
but parallels the extent to which humans consider them to be
integral to, and yet threatening to, their history.

4 The 'Hero of Science'

Science treats the rat as vermin but also presents it as the hero/heroine of science (perhaps we should say that the former enables the latter). This is a long history of victimhood, doomed heroism or martyrdom: the rat has been dissected, vivisected, electrocuted, given diseases, drowned, genetically manipulated, controlled at a distance by radio signals, and sent into outer space. If, as we have noted throughout this book, the rat shadows the human, in science this is a much more tightly conceived substitution. For the mapping to take place the rat has to be created, or recreated, by science. The commonplace that the rat is an ideal experimental animal contains within it the fact that science has created this ideal, while in turn also constructing itself, literally so in the case of laboratory equipment and housing, around its creation.

From the first recorded rat dissection, by Theophilus Müller and Johann Farber in 1621, to the publication of the genome map for *Rattus norvegicus* in 2004, just under four centuries of rat science have produced information on everything from anatomical structure and genetics to illnesses such as cancer and heart disease, from the workings of the nervous system to information on learning, emotion and memory. Rat-based science has flourished in the twentieth century, to some extent founded on one of the distinctive particularities of the rat, its fecundity and rapid rate of development. The possibility of breeding large numbers of rats for experiments combined with its size and manageability make it a perfect laboratory animal. The mass production of rats to feed a multi-billion pound industry, by means of massive and highly specialized breeding networks, makes the rat more of a cog in a machine than an animal.

Robert Boyle's essay 'New experiments physico-mechanical touching the spring of air and its effects' (1660) describes how he placed a number of creatures in his air-pump and watched the effects of the extraction of air on them. He performed this initially on two birds and a mouse.[1] He expected 'that an animal used to life in narrow holes with very little fresh air would endure the want of it better than the lately mentioned birds'. However, the mouse fairly quickly succumbed and was later dissected to determine the impact of suffocation on its inner organs. Although this is not a rat example, the elements of this early systematic experiment on a rodent presages something of what is to come: the controlled environment; a small but lively creature of a convenient size for experimental devices; a repetitious process (that in this instance is oddly playful); and death. In the early nineteenth century the first scientific work on rats, apart from anatomical drawings, focused on food and oxygen deprivation. A certain number of ad hoc experiments on rats are also reported. In 1837 a chemist named Sheldon wrote to *The Times* stating that he had brought a rat close to death with a dose of prussic acid and then revived it by pouring water down its back for several minutes and placing it by the fire. This method, he felt, may be 'successfully used to recover persons who have taken prussic acid'.[2] In 1856 animal keepers at the Jardin des Plantes in Paris produced the first recognized colony of black hooded rats, though the colony was also used to feed the reptile collection. In the same year important medical experiments on rats were carried out by the French scientist Philipeaux. He studied the effects of removing their adrenal glands, work that anticipated one of the major uses to which rats were to be put, namely endocrinology (the study of secretions by the endocrine glands). Tissue transplants in rats were practised as early as 1863 but also flourished at the turn of the century. An increased interest in the breeding of rats began to make its mark toward the end of the nineteenth century, beginning with Crampe's work using albino and wild rats in Germany between 1877 and 1885. The tying-in of breeding to scientific experiment was a key development because it heralded the possibility of using similar types of rat in repeated experiments.[3]

Work on rats accelerated during the 1890s in both medical research and psychology. Rats were used by C. C. Stewart from 1894 onwards at Clark University in the United States as part of an investigation into the effect of alcohol, diet and barometric changes on animal activity. Wild rats were placed on revolving drums and their rates of revolution measured. A year later, finding wild rats difficult to handle, Stewart switched to the more malleable albino rats.[4] It was also during the early 1890s that rats became used in neuroanatomical studies at the University of Chicago.[5] However, in the period up to 1915, scientists working with albino rats in America, Austria and Germany saw them as only one of several species useful to laboratory science. Rats, dogs, frogs and rabbits all had different advantages. The perceived advantages of rats were their ease of handling and quick reproductivity. As Henry H. Donaldson wrote in his 1915 monograph on the rat, 'albinos are clean, gentle, easily kept and bred, and not expensive to maintain . . . The rat takes . . . exercise voluntarily and is susceptible to training.

It is also highly resistant to the usual wound-infecting organisms. For a number of lines of study therefore, the rat seems to be a peculiarly suitable animal.'[6] They also developed more slowly than say, guinea pigs, with some physiological changes occurring later in life over a longer time span, thus enabling easier study of development. They were also of key interest in the study of sexuality.

In 1894 Eugen Steinach published a series of experiments on the reproductive endocrinology of white rats by removing the prostate, the vas deferens and the seminal vesicles without destroying their sex drive. When they had recovered he described their post-operative sexual potency as so intense (up to 60 matings an hour under some circumstances) that it 'bordered on the unbelievable'.[7] Steinach claimed that he could rejuvenate ageing men by vasectomy, but other important work, having its basis in rats and guinea pigs, involved changing sexual characteristics by transplanting sexual organs. His question was whether the secretions of the sex glands were sex specific or whether, for instance, the testes would intensify femininity in a female. He also transplanted ovaries into castrated males. His feminized male rats did show some bodily features of the female as well as showing a characteristic defensive reflex of the female: the raising of a hind foot and backstrike to rebuff the unwanted attentions of a male. Masculinized females also showed predatory sexual behaviour towards other females.[8] Later Steinach would stress the importance of *Mus decumanus* (the brown rat), which he would claim he was the first to use, in this work. He also used albinos, as well as crossing some with young sewer rats. He wrote, 'I feel I am not only fulfilling a debt of gratitude towards the rat but contributing something towards its rehabilitation and recognition by taking this opportunity to protest against the prejudice of the public towards these, my favourite test animals'.[9] Freud underwent one of Steinach's operations in 1923 in his efforts to fight cancer.

One historian has noted that the increasingly complicated apparatus and techniques used in the laboratory in the late nineteenth century 'tended to objectify the experiments and direct attention away from the animal itself'.[10] Around the turn of the century psychologists such as Linus Kline and Willard Small began publishing work on rats in mazes and puzzle boxes. Kline's puzzle box required an animal to dig through sawdust or break a strip of paper to enter and get food. The mechanistic methods of psychologists produced scientific results that were to be extrapolated to explaining human behaviour. Thus, the precise kind of animal in the maze was less important than behavioural sequences and efficiency of problem solving. It paralleled the idea that modernity is marked by the speeding up of time and the diminishing of space through advances in technology and transport.[11] As an increasingly integral cog to the scientific machine, the rat was not only used in experiments to examine the efficiency of motor strategies, as measured by the time taken to do things, but also represented forms of acceleration in its own right due

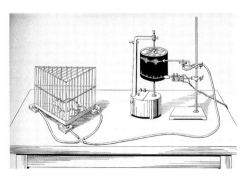

Tambour-Mounted-Cage for measuring movement in time.

to its breeding and growth rates. In the second edition of his monograph on the rat in 1924, Donaldson wrote that he did not want to convey the impression that the rat is a 'bewitched prince' nor that 'man is an overgrown rat', but he noted that they have many similarities. In fact, rats are a speeded-up version of the human: 'the nervous system of the rat grows in the same manner as that of man – only some thirty times as fast'.

The story of the standardization of the laboratory rat resembles the twentieth-century story of factory farming, as the rat increasingly became a sophisticated factory product.[12] When Donaldson moved to the Wistar Institute in Philadelphia in 1906, he began his efforts to standardize the albino rat. Parallel efforts had been going on in Europe. In 1909 Donaldson visited zoologist Hans Przibram's Institute for Experimental Biology in Vienna, which had also been breeding animals for science, including rats from about 1904.[13] It is estimated that almost half of all laboratory rats are direct descendants of the inmates at Wistar. Not only were strains of rats developed at Wistar, but a great deal of work was done on the management of conditions, care and diet of laboratory rats. Helen Dean King, another scientist at Wistar, began inbreeding albino rats in 1909. By 1920 these rats were kept in two separate lines and had reached the thirty-eighth generation of brother-sister matings. Some of King's scientific papers included observations on 25,000 rats.[14] Standardization also meant regularization and optimization for conditions of breeding, in other words control at all levels of life. A twelve-hour cycle of light (6 a.m.–6 p.m.) and darkness (6 p.m.–6 a.m.) regularized the reproduction of albino rats, which also meant greater predictibility in controlling the breeding cycle. 'By this method the rats display more regular oestrus cycles, and as a rule come into heat in about 2–3 hours after 6 a.m. on the fourth day.'[15] The connection between the rat and the machine component seemed to haunt organizational thinking at Wistar, with its interest in the 'efficient production of large numbers of quality controlled animals'.[16] The 1910 Director's Report reflected this when the Director, Milton Greenman, used as an example of efficiency the standardization of screw threads. These were developed in 1864 primarily to standardize American railroad lines and equipment. This is an unintentionally resonant figure: not only is the rat like a standard screw or bolt, but it is closely linked to the transportation networks whose increasing efficiency enabled the spread of rats as much as it did human commerce.

Although we have the beginnings of breeding standardization in the early twentieth century it was a long time before rats were produced under what we would now see as strict conditions. For the first half of the twentieth century rats could as easily come from fanciers and other kinds of rat breeders.[17] In fact, the early interest in rat strains developed as much from an interest in Mendelian inheritance (the early study of genetics and hybridity) as from the need to produce rats with reproducible characteristics that could be used in laboratories around the world. This was paralleled in the world of mice. Between 1900 and 1910 Lucien Cuenot and William Bateson in England initiated the first experiments in mice coat colour genetics. In the United States similar work was done by William Castle from 1910 with studies based on thousands of rats. His 1914 essay on piebald rats analysed colour patterns in 25,000 rats.[18] Castle also often obtained new strains of mice through his dealings with mouse fanciers whose own breeding programmes occasionally threw up unusual creatures. Harvard mouse researchers similarly co-operated with the mouse fancy by exhibiting their special mice at the local Boston shows in return for samples of new or existing mutants.[19]

Some of the main rat production companies were founded in the mid-twentieth century, including Charles River in 1947 and Carworth in 1935. Harlan Sprague-Dawley Inc., founded in 1931, began by breeding wild rats taken from a company dump.[20] Early facilities for the commercial breeding of rats were usually wooden structures with wood or concrete floors, and screened windows and doors for ventilation. There was, in other words, little in the way of strict environmental control, such as one sees in today's production of the laboratory rat.[21] Nevertheless this is the period in which rats began to be 'created', to use the word from the advertising of rat products by Charles River.[22]

Harvesting stem cells from a laboratory rat for research purposes.

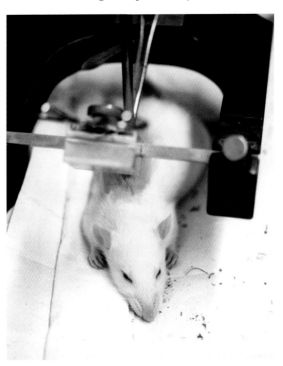

The current products are wide ranging. Consomic rats, for example, are inbred rats susceptible to cardiovascular disease into which chromosomes are transferred from cardiovascular-disease resistant rats one at a time in a series. This means that one can track the effects of different chromosomes in express-ing or repressing particular traits across a number of rats that are in all other respects genetically the same. Hence, under certain conditions, such as being fed a high salt diet, some of these rats will display hypertension and others will not, depending on the presence or absence of a particular chro-mosome. Other rat products include transgenic rats which carry additional copies of mutant or normal genes; knockout rats in which particular genes are removed or switched off; aged rats that are predisposed to spontaneous tumours, cataracts and other forms of degeneration; or nude rats, with little or no hair, that are T-cell deficient, and thus useful for tumour studies of skin and the central nervous system. These rats require highly technologized and controlled environ-ments, both for their production and in the isolation units where they are stored for laboratory experiment. Immuno-deficient rats need to be transported in completely sterile environments; they are packed in containers that are irradi-ated prior to packing and fed irradiated and sterilized food. Cryogenic freezing is also important and frozen rat ova and embryos are sold in quantity. Rats can also be sold with fur-ther modification such as various forms of implants (catheters and other devices) or with parts of their organs such as liver or pancreas removed. As the rat has become increasingly manipulated for particular scientific goals, what was once a relatively cheap and prolific animal has come to require an extensive investment in caging and maintenance. The requirements for Specific Pathogen Free or immunodeficient

A specially-bred hairless lab rat.

rats demands a level of isolation that make them some of the most controlled creatures on the planet.[23]

The history of the creation of laboratory rats in the twentieth century has produced increasing varieties of animal while exploiting its particular susceptibilities. In 1913 Johannes Fibiger

Rats in an anechoic chamber being exposed to microwave radiation as part of mobile phone research.

induced cancerous growth in rats. In 1920 it was discovered that rats fed on tapeworm eggs developed liver cancer, which furthered the possibility that the pathological vulnerabilities of the rat could be predicted and exploited. Subsequently researchers have developed all manner of rats that suffer from specific diseases. The Fischer 344 rat, for instance, spontaneously develops

Rats as an essential part of a cancer research lab, Buffalo, New York, 1909.

An x-ray of a rat.

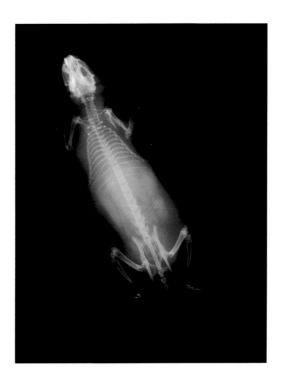

leukaemia and prostate cancer. In 1963 researchers inbreeding Wistar rats managed to produce a spontaneously hypertensive rat that could be used in the study of blood pressure and drug development for hypertension. Another significant development since the 1960s has been the development of pathogen-free strains of rats, giving one greater control over the effects of pathogens with which one can infect the rat's body.

There is a much quoted remark from 1938 by the American psychologist Edward Tolman to the effect that 'everything important in psychology (except such matters as the building of a super-ego, that is everything save such matters as involve

A rat being
trained to locate
landmines,
Tanzania, 2003.

society and words) can be investigated in essence through the
continued experimental and theoretical analysis of the deter-
miners of rat behaviour at a choice point in the maze'.[24] Rat
experiments reveal the fundamental laws of behaviour, intelligence and motivation unhindered by cultural transmission
and the variabilities of human behaviour. Once these laws are
established, they can then be applied as the basis of behaviour
in living creatures including humans. The rat is an instrument,
or perhaps one component in a larger instrument, for quanti-
fying responses to stimuli. This kind of psychology sees the rat
as a stripped down version of the human, bare of the things
taken as constituting the distinctiveness of humanity, such as
language and culture.

In 1907 John B. Watson published a monograph that examined the behaviour in a maze of rats that had been deprived of

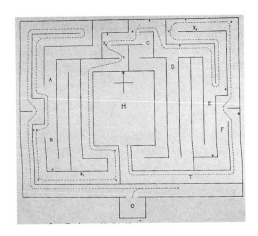

A diagram of 'Watson's maze', used in behavioural research.

some or all of their sensory organs. As a teacher in 1899, before his academic career, Watson had impressed his pupils with rats he had tamed and trained to perform various tricks.[25] For Watson, experiments done by physiologists on animals did not explain the effects of those operations 'upon the instinctively and habitually organized reactions of the animal as a whole', a lack he intended to make up for with his 'psychological' method. Watson also felt that this work had relevance for humans and put animal experiments on a par with 'the study of human defective minds and the minds of children'.[26] Having blinded a number of rats, Watson noted that their reactions seemed to be no different from normal rats, and concluded that vision plays no part in maze association.[27] Some of his anosmic rats – rats deprived of smell – also learned the maze in normal time. So he concluded that there was something that enabled the rat to learn the maze other than the sensory organs. This he labelled the kinaesthetic sense: a general inward bodily sense of orientation (an internal feedback sending information to the brain by receptors in the joints and muscles). To test this, he deprived a rat of its eyes, its olfactory bulbs, and its vibrissae – the whiskers that are so essential to the rat's sense of touch. At first this rat did not show signs of moving quickly round the maze or eating the food. However, when this rat was deprived of food until he had completed his daily quota of trips through the maze, this worked well: 'he began at once to learn the maze and finally became the usual automaton'.[28] In the end the increasing efficiency of the 'automaton' was measured by the time taken to do its task. Once the rat had learned the task, which entailed the development of a complex motor habit, it was unaffected by external stimuli.[29]

What is interesting about Watson's experiments is not so much the conclusions he draws as what this work tells us about what the rat stands for. Watson's rat is more of a unit than an animal. Furthermore, the maze experiment does not simply explain how creatures explore and come to understand their way round a new environment. It involves the creation of a new organism, one reduced to the minimum of its senses. This organism mirrors, or *embodies*, the minimum elements of behaviour: cut up, segmented and reassembled around the idea of an inner sense of movement. In order to measure and translate the elements of behaviour across species in ways that made sense meant that it was not the particular behaviours themselves that were seen as important but rather the rates at which they were done or repeated. The behaviourist B. F. Skinner, who followed in Watson's footsteps, thought that the behaviour of rats in his experimental boxes, pressing the right lever for a food pellet at certain rates, might tell us something about human learning.[30] However, despite the fact that the rat is treated as an 'abstract device', it still determines the scale of the analysis and radically restricts and simplifies the range of

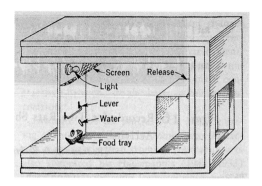

behaviours it is possible to analyse. It seems somehow significant that Robert Yerkes, a contemporary of Watson's who wrote
on animal psychology particularly in primates, should have
had his childhood pet albino rat stuffed and kept for the rest
of his life.[31] It is as if psychology is itself infantilized by the
mazes, wheels, simple geometrical shapes and electric shock
devices. From this perspective, the scientific treatment of the
rat seems not so far away from the apparatuses of the culture
of pet-keeping, the world of toys, or the playful sporting element of hunting rats.

After the First World War the rat became essential to psychology departments right across America. One American
scientist noted with alarm in 1950 that psychologists were ded-
icating over 50 per cent of their research on an animal that
represented only 0.001 per cent of the types of creatures that
might be studied.[32] One of the most useful and revealing
summary texts on psychology and rats in the mid-twentieth
century is Norman Munn's *Handbook of Psychological Research
on the Rat* (1950). This was a reworking of a book published in
1933, but the enormous expansion of work on the rat between
1933 and 1950 necessitated a fourfold increase in the literature,

requiring a bibliography of some 2,500 references. This comprehensive account of work on rats, from which I can only draw a small sample, reveals the links between violence, the control of behaviour, and scientific understanding very clearly. In this book, in an echo of Watson's maze work, are numerous experiments in which parts of the brain are removed, or lesions produced in the brain, to see how these effect things such as copulation or diurnal rhythms. In experiments done by Frank Beach in 1942, for instance, it was found that 'no inexperienced animal deprived of more than one form of sensitivity attempted copulation . . . all sexually experienced males continued to copulate after elimination of one or two senses, but the experienced copulator deprived of three failed to copulate further'. This proved the contention that neither vision, olfaction or superficial cutaneous sensitivity is essential for mating.[33] Another type of experiment involved rats being made to run on revolving drums. The scientist Carl Richter reported instances where female rats reached a daily record of 27 miles on a revolving wheel.

It is almost impossible to get a summary overview on the countless experiments carried out with rats in the twentieth century. Many of these experiments resonate with other non-scientific preoccupations with rats. This does not just apply to the kinds of physically oriented sciences we have been looking at so far, but also in other areas such as psychotherapy and psychoanalysis, where a preoccupation with the rat is often a powerful expression of childhood trauma. American psychiatrist Leonard Shengold made a series of studies of patients he labelled 'rat people'. These patients, who had been abused or overstimulated in inappropriate ways in their childhoods, had become fixated with rats, perhaps because of some association made during the period of trauma. What is interesting is the different levels at which this rattishness is expressed. On the one hand there is an obvious preoccupation with teeth and eating: 'these people spoke and thought in the language of cannibalism'.[34] On the other, the figure of the rat as victim also seems to be present, and these people often tend to turn their aggression inwards on themselves. The rat is thus both torturer and victim. In keeping with the idea of the rat as a breaker of boundaries, Shengold noted how the 'rat people' wanted to tear the analyst apart with their teeth, while at the same time craving the care of the analyst. Thus he wrote that the syndrome transcended diagnostic categories. This uncanny fluidity of the rat is reflected in a remark in a later article: 'the rat can stand either for subject or object, part-subject or part-object'.[35] The rat roams free across the different boundaries of the human body. 'The rat is a tooth carrier, endowed with the power to creep back and forth from level to level of libidinal development, from one erogenous zone to the other, biting and being bitten.'[36]

In psychotherapy and psychoanalysis the rat functions in two ways. First, it is a creature whose features, often exaggerated, can be mapped onto the human around ideas of, for example, gnawing, victimhood, dirt or fecundity. Second, it is associated with the dissolution of boundaries, the inhabiting of networks and semi-obscurity. These are features of the rat that do not map on to the idea of the human, but rather destabilize it. However, at all levels of association the rat is characterized by a certain violence or sadism. Freud's *Notes Upon A Case of Obsessional Neurosis* (1909), commonly known as the 'Rat Man' case, is a very neat example of this and worth examining from the perspective of the rat.

There are three pertinent themes in Freud's analysis: torture, rats and networks, and money. One of the main stories told to Freud by the Rat Man, whose real name was Ernst

Lehrs, concerns a tale he hears, while on military manoeuvres, of an Oriental torture. Rats are put beneath an upturned bowl on a prisoner's buttocks and the rats then bore their way into the anus.[37] He also tells a confused story of how he loses his pince-nez and when a new pair are sent from Vienna he gets entangled in a bizarre set of actions in an effort to pay the postal charge, which has been paid for him by somebody else. Ernst plans to take a journey to a lieutenant to whom he believes he owes the money by travelling to his billet in a neighbouring village and then taking a three-hour train journey to the post office before taking a train to Vienna. The fact that Ernst then gets stuck in a network of railways and time-tables makes him like a rat in a maze. Eventually, he gets on the Vienna train thinking at every stop he will get out and make the journey in the opposite direction. He never does and ends up in Vienna where, in the end, he simply sends the money to the post office.[38] The stories Ernst tells lead to a series of proliferating associations in which rats are likened to money through a number of etymological links, as well as to other things as the case study proceeds: children, aspects of anal eroticism, worms, the penis, syphilis, dirt, and even marriage.[39] 'Rats had acquired a series of symbolic meanings to which, during the period which followed, fresh ones were continually being added.'[40] The association of rats and money occurs throughout the case study. There is a link between *ratten* (rats) and *raten* (instalments) and on a number of occasions Ernst likens rats to coins.[41] Even syphilis was given a rat-like quality, as it was associated with the gnawing and eating of the body.[42] When pointing out that the rat was a penis, Freud noted that this produced a 'whole flood of associations'.[43] The rat means almost everything of any powerful significance in Ernst's mental universe.

What emerges from this set of associations is the idea that the rat represents an almost plague-like eruption of symbols starting with its first appearance as part of a torture and then as a rat-borne contagion (of ideas) that brings the rat by rail to Vienna with all the manifest ills that Freud will need to cure. This might be stretching the allegorical links with the rat, but it does echo the manner in which rats are poisonous objects in circulation around transport networks, something very pertinent to the years of bubonic plague from the mid-1890s. The dangers of railways are also emphasized when Ernst believes that Freud is related to Leopold Freud, a notorious train murderer from Budapest. However, a very direct link is made by Freud between the rat and the idea of the network. In his case notes on the Rat Man he remarks that the rat story is a nodal point (*knotenpunkt*) which relates to remarks he made earlier in the *Studies on Hysteria* about chains of ideas. 'The logical chain corresponds not only to a zig-zag, twisted line, but rather to a ramifying system of lines and more particularly to a converging one. It contains nodal points at which two or more threads connect and thereafter proceed as one; and as a rule several threads that run independently.'[44] If rats circulate in these (railway-like) networks and accrue meanings as they go, they become like a type of currency suffering from galloping inflation, a symbolic epidemic.[45]

The third notion in Freud returns us to the theme of sadism and violence that we have seen as characterizing the position of the rat in science more generally. In a letter to Wilhelm Fliess written in 1897 Freud had likened psychoanalysis to torture, and the Rat Man case is full of fantasies of violence, the worst of which are in the case notes rather than in the published case study.[46] If Ernst represents, momentarily in his life at any rate, a hybrid of rat and man then the monstrous acts of violence would somehow reflect that particular incarnation, especially round things connected to disgust, gnawing and penetration. Although Freud in the published version focuses on Ernst's relations with his father, the violent fantasies in relation to women in the case notes require some attention. At one point Ernst imagines Freud's mother naked with two swords sticking into her breast with the 'lower part of her body and especially her genitals . . . entirely eaten up by me [i.e. Freud] and the children'.[47] On another occasion Ernst dreamt that he was lying on his back on a girl (Freud's daughter) and was copulating with her by means of the stool hanging from his anus. Through all these fantasies the symbolic links with rats take them to extremes of disgust which Freud will do his best to contain, and, by drawing attention away from these figures of women and focusing on the father figure, he neutralizes and rationalizes them.[48] There is, around the figure of the rat, a set of extremes which mirrors that of science, in which the interdependency of control and violence suggest that the poles of order and disorder are very close and at times interchangeable. Does the mapping of human onto rat epitomize a problem of identity or is it a way of satisfying a sadistic impulse? Characteristically, the rat allows for both.

The final strand in the history of the rat in science is where the rat is no longer simply an interchangeable body but part of a system in which body parts are themselves interchangeable. In 2002, for instance, *New Scientist* reported two experiments involving rats which illustrate this strikingly. In one the teeth of pigs were grown in the abdomen of rats. The tooth buds of these six-month-old pigs developed into molars but formed no roots. In another experiment infant rats were decapitated and their heads grafted onto the thighs of adults. This research was intended to elucidate problems that arise from blood loss to the brain in newborn humans. In the right conditions the rat brain was able to develop as normal for three weeks with the mouth reported as moving as if trying to drink milk.[49] Here the rat body becomes a monstrous hybrid in which it is no longer clear where the rat begins and ends. If these instances reveal the biological interchangeability of the rat, a further step is where the rat becomes integrated with technology.

Scientist Sanjiv Talwar has run a project in New York in which rats are controlled by radio waves via electrodes implanted in the brain. A radio receiver on the rat receives controlling instructions from a computer. One electrode is implanted in that part of the brain responsible for sensing reward, while two others are connected to the parts that receive stimulation from the left and right whiskers. A radio receiver receives instruction by computer issuing controls to the rat. Rats were placed in mazes as well as open environments, including pipes, ledges and collapsed piles of concrete rubble. Because the rat gets its feeling of reward directly by stimuli to the brain rather than having to respond to certain cues for its rewards, this was felt to be a highly efficient way of instigating learning. The future of this technology envisages an increasingly complex version of rat and machine. 'It may also be possible to increase the "bandwidth" of conditionable information by stimulating multiple brain sites, thereby increasing the variety of reactions that can be elicited . . . a guided rat can be developed into an effective "robot" that will possess several natural advantages over current mobile robots. Moreover, the ability to receive brain sensory activity remotely and interpret it accurately could allow a guided rat to function as both a mobile robot and a biological sensor.'[50] An even more radical hybridization of rat and machine has been produced by the Symbiotica Fish and Chips Project.

A rat-brain neuron, magnified 170 times.

This project began with the growing of fish neurons over silicon chips but more recently an art installation known as MEART has been created which uses neurons from an embryonic rat cortex grown over a multi-electrode array. These cells are connected to a computer and are stimulated by information provided by a webcam, which in turn is filming visitors in a gallery. A recording is made from the stimulated neurons and this sends signals to a robotic arm that creates the imagery. As the website describing this notes, 'the uniqueness of MEART is the attempt to create an intelligent artificial/biological artist that has in itself the capability or potential to be creative. We are focusing on creating the artist rather than the artwork. MEART proposes to embody the fusion of biology and the machine – creativity emerging from a semi-living entity.'[51] In this instance the rat neurons are in a laboratory in Atlanta, Georgia, and the robotic arm is in Perth, Western Australia. At one level this is an extreme version of the rat/machine

As part of a project to research environmental feedback and learning, rat neurons control the movements of a 'hybrot' arm that then draws pictures (Multi-Electrode Array aRT); the neurons receive input back, so that they can 'see' what they've drawn.

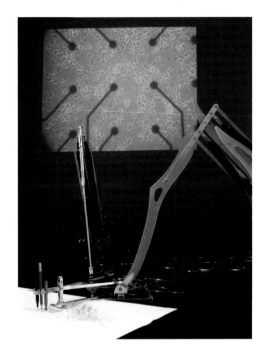

interface where the body is completely disarticulated from the function of its parts, and it probably makes little sense to talk of the rat in this instance. However, it reminds us in a bizarre way that rats, as I have said throughout this book, are the totem animal of modernity. And in that sense it comes as little surprise that they should so readily be turned into machines that straddle the globe.

The most recent development in rat science at the time of writing is the publication of 90 per cent of the genome of *Rattus norvegicus* at the end of March 2004. This genetic map revealed that rats have been evolving at a faster rate than humans, about three times as fast, and that they have developed extraordinarily in their sense of smell (they have an estimated 2,070 smell receptor genes, one-third more than in mice) as well as an ability to deal more effectively with toxins in their liver. However, prior advances in mouse genetics had made the latter the preferred research animal. From the late 1980s gene knockout technology, which created breeds of mice with a single gene taken out, and subsequent developments where genes could be 'knocked in' again, made the mouse a more significant animal. Until very recently it has been much more difficult to isolate stem cells and clone rats. The first transgenic rat was created in Germany in 1990 with an additional gene that causes high blood pressure and the first cloned rat, Ralph, was created in 2003.[52] Overall rodents and humans are close genetically: 'the broad similarity in the number, order and sequence of genes between rodents and humans is reassuring, as is the fact that as many as 90% of rat genes have matches in both humans and mice'.[53] The rat has 2.75 billion pairs of base DNA, the mouse 2.6 billion and humans 2.9 billion.[54]

The numbers of rats used in science during the twentieth century has been countless. To take a small sample from a single country, in 1978, of the 5.2 million animals experimented on in Britain, over 4 million were rats and mice.[55] In 1993 it was noted that animal experiments ran at some 3.5 million procedures a year with rodents the most commonly used.[56] In 2002 the number of animals used for the first time in procedures was 2.66 million, with rats making up 19 per cent and mice 63 per cent. At one level the 'rat's image has been transformed from plague carrier to indispensable tool in experimental medicine and drug development', although the history of experimentation has more than enough examples which implicitly cast them as vermin worthy of few welfare considerations.[57] A 1980 experiment studying the influence of stress on the initiation of cancer subjected rats to a six-hour exposure to a temperature of −6°C; amputation of the leg; electric shock; exposure to flashing lights for eight hours daily; induction of convulsions and so on.[58] A 1962 experiment gave electric shocks to rats when they fought, which led to one pair receiving 18,000 shocks over seven and a half hours.[59] Michael Lynch has written that there are two kinds of rat: analytic and naturalistic.[60] The first is the rat created by science, that is in many respects a set of abstract data, and the second the one we know from common-sense experience. However, as much of the material in this book has shown, almost all experience of the rat is mediated through particular cultural responses to it. If we look at some of the elements that make up the scientific construction of the rat, marked profligacy, excess, the darker side of the human psyche, and shadowed by disease and violence, then we are not that far away from those 'commonplace' responses to the rat that constitute other parts of our experience of them.

5 Plague and Pollution

About 70 diseases are carried by the rat. Aside from bubonic plague, they include rabies, typhus, leptospirosis, trichinosis, tularaemia, rat-bite fever, and diseases associated with the Hanta virus. However, the disease most linked to rats and which has had the greatest cultural impact on humans in history is bubonic plague. Attitudes to bubonic plague parallel attitudes to rats themselves. Though it is not necessarily the most lethal disease in terms of death rate it is one that often strikes the most fear, much in the way that the rat is often the most hated animal. In the period between 1896 and 1914, 8 million people in India died from plague. But malaria and tuberculosis killed double that figure; smallpox and cholera were devastating; and influenza killed twice as many as plague in just four months between 1918 and 1919. As one historian notes of the Indian epidemic that began in Bombay in 1896, 'no other epidemic evoked the fear and panic generated by plague'.[1] The scale of fear is epitomized by the first telegram report to *The Times* when plague broke out in the summer of 1894 in Hong Kong: 'half native population Hong Kong left, numbering 100,000. Leaving by 1000s daily; 1500 deaths.'[2]

The rat is a bearer of plague, but at a second degree as host to the plague-carrying flea, the direct agent of infection. In many places, such as Java, the vulnerable commensal rat can act as a carrier between wild field species, who are resistant to the disease, and human beings. The interplay between enzootic plague (where plague exists in a permanent reservoir of rodents) and epizootic plague (where it breaks out in populations and spreads), depends on variable factors such as contacts between species, seasonal breeding patterns of fleas, migrations and patterns of human settlement.[3] The Indian gerbil (*Tatera indica*), for instance, has been indentified as the endemic source in northern India and it is this that conveys the disease to the black rat.[4] Bubonic plague has been, in the main, a seasonal disease and can also strike with apparent randomness. Some households or villages can be devastated whilst other neighbouring ones can be left untouched. This was a puzzle that preoccupied many early twentieth-century investigators of plague, such as E. H. Hankin, who remarked that rats seemed to spread plague in varying degrees at different times. He also noted that there was no necessary connection between the intensity of plague and the inadequacy of sanitary conditions in dwellings. Although areas where plague was endemic, such as in parts of China and the Transbaikal, were often impoverished or barely populated, Hankin recognized that when such areas were opened up the threat of a spread of plague was increased. He noted the potential problems for plague dissemination presented by the opening up of routes like the Trans-Siberian or the Cape to Cairo railways.[5]

In her book on plague in China, Carol Benedict noted how the opium trade led to the creation of trade routes through plague bearing areas in the mid-nineteenth century.[6] Just as the rat spread through trade and transport networks so did the disease. The plague spread through the Guangxi and western Quangdong areas in the 1860s and 1870s, emerging in the Pearl River delta in the 1890s. Its subsequent outbreak in Canton and Hong Kong in 1894 led to the outbreaks in India and then, through shipping, to major ports all round the world. The exact mechanisms of the link between plague and rats were not scientifically understood until the very end of the nineteenth century. Previous to that rats had been associated with the plague only as harbingers: witnesses had long chronicled the dying rat as heralding the coming of plague. In the mid-seventeenth century it had been noted that 'packs of rats' crossed rivers in large numbers prior to the outbreak of disease. A migration of rats from the desert into Astrakan in 1727 was seen then as a portent of plague.[7] Hong Liangji, an eighteenth-century writer, described the rats that came out of the ground in Zhaozhao in the daytime, spat up blood and fell dead. People 'breathing the vapour of the dead rats' quickly became ill and died.[8]

It has long been noted in many different cultures of both East and West that animals come out of the ground before or during times of plague. The upheaval in the ground can, of course, be due to earthquakes or other natural calamities. A modern example is the San Francisco earthquake of 1906, which led to a renewed outbreak of plague in 1907, in this instance in part due to the breaking up of drains and sewers underground and the unsanitary conditions in the encampments for the survivors.[9] In China in the late nineteenth century it was felt that a pestilential energy (*qi*) passes through rat burrows on its way to the surface and drives the rats out in search of water. Humans drinking from the same containers will be contaminated by the pestilence.[10] In the Middle East both Arabic and Latin sources emphasized that the fourteenth-century Black Death was initially accompanied by violent events like floods, famine and earthquakes.[11] In his discussions of plague, the Arabic medical writer Ibn Sina noted that one sign of its approach was rats and subterranean animals fleeing to the surface of the earth and behaving as if intoxicated. Then they would die. It was believed that animals perceived the evil miasma that brought disease before humans did.[12] Similar sentiments can be found in Thomas Lodge's *Treatise on Plague* (1603): 'and when as rats, moules and other creatures (accustomed to live underground) forsake their holes and habitations, it is a token of corruption in the same'.[13]

The idea of rats and mice coming out of their holes dates back to the Arabic philosopher Avicenna, who took the view that the corruption of the world was transferred through them to humans. It is a pre-scientific viewpoint that is almost correct.[14] The plague bacillus can reside in the earth. It survives only a few days in putrefying bodies, though it can last years if the bodies are frozen. In the micro-climate of the burrows of rodents it can survive months and sometimes even years.[15] The idea that rats should be controlled and eradicated in an effort to control plague is found in some contexts prior to the post-1894 epidemics, although it is not claimed that rats are directly responsible for plague. Sir Theodore de Mayerne, who in 1631 presented a report to Charles I on plague prevention in London, was unique in thinking that 'rats, mice, weasels and such vermin' were among the carriers of plague.[16] The more common view in seventeenth-century England was that the abundance of mice and rats was a portent of plague.

Charles Creighton, in his extensive *History of Epidemics in Britain* (1891–4), cites a number of passages from reports on plague in rural areas in India and China between the 1850s and the 1870s, in which filthy living conditions, inadequate disposal of bodies, and the dying of rats prior to outbreaks were all noted features. The fact that humans and rats shared the sickness only implied for Creighton that it emanated from living conditions, particularly where people shared their houses with cattle, although the cattle were not themselves affected. In one group of plague-stricken villages in India the houses were, literally, embedded in dung.

On the ground floor herd the cattle; in this compartment the dung is allowed to accumulate until such time as there is no room left for the cattle to stand erect; it is then removed and carefully packed around all sides, so that the house literally stands in the centre of a hot bed . . . In many instances we have seen it accumulated above the level of the floor of the upper story in which the family lives.[17]

In a report on the same area published in 1877 the manner in which rats died prior to the outbreak of human plague seemed quite particular:

in the houses of families about to suffer from an outbreak of plague, rats are sometimes found dead on the floor. Planck had seen them himself; all that he had seen appeared to have died suddenly, as by suffocation, their bodies being in good condition, a piece of rag sometimes clenched in the teeth.

In another report from Yunnan in 1878, the rats would 'leave their holes in troops and after staggering about and falling over each other, drop down dead'. Or they would spring 'continually upwards from their hind legs as if they were trying to jump out of something'.

It took a while for the association of rats with plague and the mechanism by which plague was actually transferred to humans to be understood. In 1894 Yersin and Roux had written that the plague was an illness of the rat.[18] Ogata's experiments, published in 1897, successfully infected mice by injecting them with the crushed fleas of rats that had died of plague. In a series of experiments published in 1898, the French scientist Simond managed to prove that fleas were the vector of infection. Having failed to get animals infected by mere contact, he suspended a rat in a cage in a bottle which in turn contained a flea-ridden rat dying of plague. Eventually the second rat died.[19] To understand the role of the rat in the dissemination of plague required the suspension of a number of preconceptions about the causes of plague. In India the Indian Plague Commission resisted the implications of Simond's thesis because it 'undermined the assumptions connecting hypotheses about the nature of the disease to notions of social behaviour and cultural characteristics in India, upon which epidemiological work had been preceding'.[20] Because plague was for many associated with filth and poverty, as well as assumptions about the class and race of its victims, attempts to prevent the disease on the basis of such ideas ironically made it worse. The removal of roofs and the flooding of houses or sewers with disinfectant simply drove the rats elsewhere. The effectiveness of such disinfection was undermined by experiments, for instance in 1906 in Bombay, in which guinea pigs were released into disinfected houses and still picked up fleas. In fact, much of the work confirming the rat–flea hypothesis was done during the outbreaks in Sidney in 1900 and 1902.[21]

Professional rat-catchers during the outbreak of bubonic plague in Sydney, 1900.

I have claimed in this book that the rat is one of the totem animals of modernity. Both the spread of plague and, eventually, the methods used to control the rat bear this out. The reason India suffered such a high mortality (95 per cent of the global plague mortality between 1895 and 1939) was a 'peculiar amalgam of modernization and underdevelopment'. Its modern transport system, extensive grain trade, high human mobility and large commensal rat populations all contributed.[22] The differential distribution of plague was also affected by the types of rodents. Bombay, with its huge black rat population and high densities of the *Xenopsylla cheopis* flea, the species of flea most significant for plague epidemics, suffered greatly compared to Calcutta, whose major rodent was the bandicoot, which lived less close to humans and was less of a host to the *X. cheopis* flea. Madras and southern India generally also suffered less, partly because the dominant flea, *X. astia*, was an inferior plague carrier, and partly because the hotter climatic conditions were less favourable to the disease.

Once rats became the source of intensive study, the systematic surveillance and control of rat populations had an assembly line quality. Traps, when filled, were taken to depots, where detailed forms were filled describing things like location and species of rat. Traps were then placed in a heavy canvas bag and sent to the laboratory. It had been noticed that when traps were sent to the laboratory in sunlight the fleas would drop off the rats. The traps and the bags were chloroformed and the fleas counted for each trap. Lines of men stood at long trestle tables processing the rats, counting fleas, doing post-mortems and entering the results on detailed forms. As a perusal of the plague studies in the *Journal of Hygiene* reveals, especially from 1906 onwards, a huge amount of statistical information about rats, fleas, mortality rates, climate and geographical information was collated.

Bubonic plague struck Bombay between 1896 and 1914; although a full understanding of the transmission mechanism was then undeveloped, medical authorities were trapping rats to count and examine fleas; the traps are enclosed in canvas bags to prevent escapes.

Flea-counting and rat dissection in Bombay during the 1890s–1900s plague.

Rat-counting in Bombay today.

One emergent pattern was that outbreaks of the disease in the brown rat, that lived more in drains and gulleys, often preceded outbreaks in the black rat, that lived in walls and roofs; this in turn was followed by human infection.

The plague outbreaks in San Francisco between 1900 and 1908 offer an interesting picture of the manner in which shifting attitudes to, and control measures for, the rat involved shifts of ideas around the racial character of the disease. The first plague fatality in San Francisco's Chinatown in March 1900, shortly after the beginning of the Year of the Rat, led to a series of measures that initially sealed off Chinatown and led to fears that anti-Chinese sentiment would turn into something much more dangerous. They all knew that in Honolulu the burning of plague houses had sparked off a fire that had destroyed the whole of Chinatown there. Certainly for many in the San Francisco press, the association of disease and migrants was a natural coupling. As one contemporary put it, 'the forces of exotic disease had beached galleys on our shores – the repulsion of the invader was the duty of our nation'.[23] In fact, the American Surgeon General, Walter Wyman, was already aware that rats were considered to be the chief agents in spreading plague from port to port, but systematic and extensive destruction of rats for plague control did not take place at this point. However, by the plague outbreak of 1907 the rat could be said to have replaced the migrant as the source of the disease, offering itself as a different type of scapegoat. Whereas in 1900 plague had been concentrated in one particular area of the city, in 1907 the cases were spread out and attacked citizens regardless of race.[24]

The outbreak in 1907 was in part due to the San Francisco earthquake and fire of April 1906. The rupturing of the city's buildings and pipeworks, coupled with large numbers of homeless in camps, created perfect conditions for rats. During this second outbreak of plague the killing and examination of rats was taken much more seriously, reflecting the final acceptance of the rat–flea hypothesis; it became the focus of a city-wide collective effort. The rat became *the* enemy: 'the massive slaughter of rodents proved almost cathartic for "can do" San Franciscans'.[25] A rattery was set up in which huge numbers of rats were dissected for post-mortem. On the walls of the rattery were fly-papers to capture insects that might fly off the carcasses, while the workers treated themselves constantly with vaccine.[26] Great care was taken to protect the skinners of rats, and the carcasses were immersed in a 'corrosive sublimate' before being tacked onto shingles. Rats were forwarded in galvanized iron cans. Hundreds of rats were dissected every day and their corpses burnt after examination. The scene must have been quite extraordinary, with the powerful smells of chemicals, burning rats, and production line dissection. Rupert Blue later remarked that at one point over 1,000 men were used in plague control and not a single case of plague occurred among them.[27] By the end of October 1908 the rat trapping and killing organization run by Blue had 'set over ten million pieces of bait. More than 350,000 rats had been trapped, killed and collected from bounty hunters. Over 154,000 animals had undergone bacteriologic tests at the Fillmore Street rattery . . . for months, San Franciscans saw great gray rafts of rat cadavers wash out of the sewers and into the bay, floating on the waves and bobbing against the rocks.'[28]

The rat as a visible symptom of plague has led to a number of assumptions about plagues prior to the nineteenth century. Even if rats were not noted by contemporary observers in earlier periods of plague it has been thought that they must have been there because it was assumed that the plagues were bubonic. Commenting on the 1771 outbreak in Moscow, John Alexander notes that Muscovites do not mention rats and assumes that that is due to the fact that rats were too commonplace to mention.[29] This is a refrain that runs through a number of studies of plague. In Jesuit accounts of plague in sixteenth-century Europe, for instance, there is not a single mention of rats.[30] References to rats in contemporary English records of seventeenth-century plague are also absent.[31] While this certainly does not prove the absence of bubonic plague, assumptions about rats are part of a certain view of plague that is strongly conditioned by late nineteenth-century experiences. Thus Michael Dols notes a 'curious failure' in the Middle East and Europe to mention the extermination of plague-carrying rodents even though in other contexts they were plentiful and a well-known nuisance.[32]

However, the failure to mention rats during the early epidemics could suggest other conclusions about the diseases involved. It would be ironic if the medieval Black Death, one of the most extensive catastrophes for which the rat is held responsible, was not in fact a rat-borne disease.[33] Samuel Cohn has argued that there is considerable evidence that the Black Death in medieval Italy does not have the hallmarks of bubonic plague. The virulence of the disease was remarkable in that it spread from the toe of Italy in December 1347 to the north of Norway by December 1350. Cohn claims that this speed of infection points to the possibility that the disease was an airborne infection. The Black Death travelled on average at about five miles per day, very much faster than the plague in South Africa during the period 1899–1925, which spread at about eight to twelve miles per year.[34] Studies of the behaviour of the rat in India also note that it stays in small territories. Captain G. I. Davys, who between 1907 and 1908 produced an extensive study of rats and the distribution of plague in an area of villages in the Punjab, concluded that there was no evidence of long distance movement by rats. As an experiment he released 500 rats into a field, but only one reached the houses 250 metres away.[35] Tied as it is to the human world, long distance migration of the rat will always be determined by the means of transport humans provide. The building of the Uganda railway between Mombasa and Kisumu between 1896 and 1901 assisted in the spread of plague, as did the line between Dar-es-Salaam and Lake Tanganyika built between 1905 and 1914, also linking previously dormant plague foci.[36] However, rats will not travel far on their own.

Samuel Cohn notes a number of other reasons why the medieval Black Death may not have been bubonic plague. First, the outbreaks in Italy were at times of the year that were not peak breeding times for fleas. The seasonality of plague is the result of narrow limits of humidity and temperature required for the breeding cycle of the flea. Too dry and hot, like the summers in Rome and Florence, and the flea disappears. But these were precisely the periods of the year that the Black Death re-emerged.[37] Second, Cohn notes that plague is not as lethal as popular opinion makes out. Less than 15 per cent of infected fleabites actually transmit the disease to humans. Gatacre, in his *Report on the Bubonic Plague* (1896–7), remarks that people who visited the sick in hospital or sat by the bedside of sick friends did not contract plague, confirming the old saying that the safest place to be in an epidemic is the plague ward.[38] Third, contemporary observers do not describe that rats were leaving their holes and dying, as occurs in plague.[39] Fourth, Cohn claims that humans have never developed an inbuilt immunity to bubonic plague – though rats have to a limited extent – whereas decreasing death rates in successive outbreaks suggest some sort of growing immunity to the Black Death.[40] Graham Twigg raises other queries in relation to the Black Death. In Britain the outdoor climate and environment is not congenial to rats, which mitigates against them being a likely factor in spreading the disease between widely dispersed country villages.[41] He also notes that buboes, the black lumps that appear under the skin in bubonic plague, can appear in other diseases such as smallpox and anthrax, and suggests anthrax as the disease of the Black Death. In Iceland there were two severe outbreaks of disease between 1402 and 1404, but the Icelandic terrain and climate were extremely inhospitable to rats and there were no wheeled vehicles, so rats would have had to travel in the baggage on pack animals, which seems unlikely. In fact, there is no archaeological evidence for rats in Iceland prior to the seventeenth century.[42]

I have spent some time on the case against the Black Death being bubonic plague not to resolve the argument, but to show that the relationship between the rat and epidemics of plague may be more complicated and uncertain than previously assumed. What the nineteenth- and twentieth-century assumptions about the Black Death reveal is the all-pervasive idea that the rat is responsible for the worst evils and catastrophes attendant on humans. 'The history of rats is tightly interwoven with the economic rise and fall of the ancient world, as well as the expansion of the medieval economy.'[43] Rats, like the disease, appear as a constraining element on human endeavour, shadowing mercantile and other forms of expansion. They become the embodiment of a constraint on human progress. Rat-borne plague threatens a certain notion of social order, one that is dependent on movement and commerce. Writing in 1924, Glen Liston called plague a 'disease of primitive civilisation', and claimed that it was through social reform that such diseases were banished: 'the civilising principles and the sanitary measures which had their unrecognised beginning in the conquest of plague'.[44] Interestingly, despite the focus on dirt as the marker of the plague threat, and the rats that went with it, dirt in itself was not necessarily the real danger. Experiments between 1898 and 1903 had shown that healthy animals could live in close contact with the excreta of plague-infected animals and not get infected.[45] However, as a disease-bearer the rat presents a double threat both as an immigrant (coming, like the plague, from the Orient) and as a danger to health. The plague-bearing rat had come to be seen as a prime cause of historical change in the Middle Ages. By the early twentieth century it not only made plague visible but became the main target for its control. It became the central focus of the bureaucratization of disease control, with the recording of addresses, the counting of fleas, the documentation of size, gender, species, leading to the assembling of large quantities of statistics. The plague-bearing rat was in that sense subject to the same system of recording and documenting that created the rat of twentieth-century science.

6 Pets, Vermin, Food

The British rat fancy was institutionalized in 1901 when rats made their first appearances in pet shows. The fancy is a term derived from fantasy and was from the early nineteenth century a collective term for hobbyists or collectors of particular things. The animal or bird fancier was seen as one whose interest was in pedigree.[1] The purpose of the rat fancy is to create rats that are the object of beauty and admiration. The fascination with breeding and creating animal varieties as an amateur hobby, rather than for purposes of agriculture or horseracing, became increasingly institutionalized in the second half of the nineteenth century through fancy societies, exhibitions and publications. The rat fancy was part of those small stock fancies that became increasingly visible in the last two decades of the nineteenth century: rabbits, cavies, song birds and mice. The movement to form a National Rabbit Club began in 1885, whilst the National Mouse Club (NMC) was established, with some initial faltering, in 1895. The pages of the journal *Fur and Feather* provide both a useful barometer of the relative health of the different fancies and a forum for debates around animal standardization and inbreeding that are key to the development of new varieties.[2] However, there were previous traditions of breeding rodents for looks. The discovery of an eighteenth-century book on mouse breeding from Japan reveals a good understanding of

An Edwardian
Christmas card
reflects the
popularity of
rats as pets.

WITH BEST WISHES FOR
CHRISTMAS AND THE NEW YEAR
FROM
E. W. RICHARDSON, *Editor,*
The Picture Postcard.

the principles of creating varieties. The book gives an account of
the origin of the Japanese albino mouse, which arrived from
China in the seventeenth century, and gives a series of breeding
instructions, such as 'from amongst black-spotted mice, choose
a pair of very slightly coloured animals, and cross them. From
among this offspring pick out the least coloured individuals and

cross them. By repeating this procedure you may eventually get black-eyed white mice.' A promised second book on breeding red, light yellow and lilac yellow mice was not discovered.[3]

The varying fortunes of the rat fancy in the twentieth century, from 1901 to the creation of the National Fancy Rat Society (NFRS) in 1976, reveal a trend towards an increasing number of different breeds and, inevitably, an improved knowledge of the genetics of colour. At the first show, held in Aylesbury, Buckinghamshire, on 23 and 24 October 1901, the one class 'Rats, any variety' was won by Miss Mary Douglas for an even marked, good size, black and white, 'shown in lovely trim'.[4] There was some criticism by the NMC of the rat exhibitors in these early days: several rats were shown in unsuitable bird cages, and exhibitors were asked to send out tame specimens 'that will not object to being handled, and keep those at home that are liable to bite'.[5] Throughout the period from 1901 until the early 1920s, largely due to the pioneering activities of Mary Douglas, 'the mother of the rat fancy', rats become an increasingly significant component in the small animal fancy.[6] One

Mary Douglas, the 'mother of the rat fancy'.

legacy of this is the long and exotic official listing of acceptable rat varieties by the NFRS as of January 2004, including breeds such as Champagne, Russian Blue, Rex, Topaz, Lilac Agouti, Argente Cream, and Platinum. A total of 61 varieties are listed in their Standards of Excellence and New Varieties with details of required criteria. The language of the rat fancy can be highly aesthetic:

left The Russian Blue fancy rat.

A pink-eyed white.

> if you introduced the pink-eyed dilution factor into blues, self-silvers would be the logical conclusion. These should, by careful selection, be different from champagnes, which have a warm tone; silvers should be lighter with an ice-blue effect . . . By crossing blues into Siamese and/or Himalayans, both blue and lilac points are a possibility.[7]

There are two aspects to the rat fancy that bear on the themes of this book. The first turns on the status of the rat fancy in relation to other animal fancies, which tells us something about the general status of the rat; the second relates to the larger question of what sort of animal is being created by the fancy. There was no doubt that in the 1890s the most popular fancy animals after dogs, cats, and birds such as pigeons and cage birds, were rabbits and cavies. A plaintive letter to *Fur and Feather* in 1895 complained that it rarely covered the subject of fancy mice and asserted that mice were convenient, clean and intelligent and 'a decided advantage to those who live in towns and whose lives are otherwise busily employed'. In other words, a perfect fancy for the modern world. A week later another letter noted the beauties of fancy mice and claimed that you can get silver greys, tortoiseshells, blues, lavenders and creams. This is a language firmly rooted in the aesthetics of ornament.[8] The mouse fancy finally gained a regular column in *Fur and Feather* in 1899 but was always dominated in terms of coverage by the larger fancies of rabbit, cat and cavies. The rat fancy in turn played something of a second fiddle to the mouse fancy; though the NMC was renamed the National Mouse and Rat Club in 1913, the phrase 'and rat' was removed in 1929. However, in the years around the First World War the rat fancy gained plenty of attention through the writings of Mary Douglas who began contributing a column entitled 'Rat Resumé' specifically on rats to *Fur and Feather* in 1912. The standards of entries by rat fanciers and the level of enthusiasm seems to have varied. In 1917 the column 'Mouse Notes' noted that 'the miserable support' by rat fanciers at recent shows had disappointed promoters and inspired the suggestion that there should be a specialist club for rats.[9]

The periods of decline of the rat fancy do not seem to bear much relation to periods in which the rat's verminous or disease ridden status comes to the fore. After all, the fancy developed during the precise period when the plague-bearing attributes of the rat were finally identified. However, there is a parallel between the rat fancy and the development of rat breeds for laboratory science; not only are they two sides of an interconnected practice, but at present fancy rats derive mainly from laboratory stock.[10] Thus scientists manipulate the rat's body for purposes of experimentation, while devotees and admirers of the rat do so for purposes of exhibition and personal satisfaction. In both instances, the aim is to create an 'ideal' rat, whatever the purpose. Issues of bodily conformation and uniform standards in the rat fancy are crucial. In general the template is that of *Rattus norvegicus*, though a *Rattus rattus* (then *Mus rattus*) was first shown at the Wadebridge show in Cornwall in 1914 by H. C. Brooke, when it was best in show. Remarking that it was more slender and elegant than the brown rat, Brooke also sounded a patriotic note. 'What more appropriate moment than the present can we choose to restore the Old English Rat, harried almost out of existence by his burly Northern cousin, to his own place again, in the world of Fancy at last.'[11] In many ways the rat fancy is in good health these days and has societies in the United States, Sweden, Finland, the Netherlands and Germany. It benefits hugely from the internet. In 2003, a World Rat Day was instituted in America as an annual event, held on 4 April. Since 1974 there has also been a Rat Olympics held at Nebraska Wesleyan University, though recently, because the term Olympics infringes the name

The rat 'Olympics', the Xtreme Rat Challenge held at Nebraska Wesleyan University.

of the US Olympics Committee, the event has been renamed 'Xtreme Rat Challenge'. Events include hurdling, rope climbing, weight lifting and the long jump.

The antithesis to these various ways of celebrating the rat is the industry devoted to their eradication. The two have at least one thing in common: total control over the birth, life and death of the rat. Books on vermin control, with their designs for traps and bait recipes, serve as a record not only of the variety of ways of dealing with rats over time but also as a reflection of attitudes towards them at different periods of history. This includes the changing categorization of acceptable and noxious animals. W. R. Boelter cites a list of vermin by a medieval writer that includes bees, spiders, silkworms, toads, gnats, fleas and lice, but not rats.[12] In 1590, Leonard Mascall published a collection of what he called 'sundrie engines and trappes', which included all manner of traps for rats and mice including one

A 15th-century rat-trap in action.

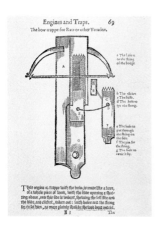

A 'bowe trappe' from Leonard Pascall's *Sundrie Engines and Trappes* (1600).

A rat-catcher is a central figure among the 'Criers of London'.

based on the design of a crossbow, a mill trap which tumbled mice into a pot of water, and a 'dragin' trap which brought a spiked collar down on the victim.[13] In a text from 1680 a list of vermin includes rats and mice, moles, pismires (ants), flies, caterpillars, snakes, weasels, bugs, frogs, and fleas and lice.[14] Recipes for poison and designs for traps are given in these books. Although rats and mice have always been killed, occasionally consideration is given to questions of acceptable and unacceptable means of killing. Catchers such as Robert Smith, in 1768, found poisons less congenial as rats would crawl away and die somewhere inaccessible, giving rise to a foul smell. Arsenic and 'corrosive sublimate' were not to be recommended.[15] Phosphorus and plaster of Paris, which expanded in the rat's stomach when it drank water, were also recognized as particularly painful poisons and not always favoured. Recipes for bait and poison varied considerably in the seventeenth and eighteenth centuries. One eighteenth-century text suggested that

A rat-catcher is part of the crowd in an etching of 1740 by C.W.E. Dietrich.

A ratcatcher (and seller of rat-traps) from Edmé Bouchardon's *Les Cris de Paris* (1746).

An undated engraving by Cornelis de Visscher of the rat-catcher with his boy assistant; the rat-catcher/boy holds poison in his right hand.

a paste made by mixing hog's lard with the brains of a weasel was a way of stopping rats coming into a room. It also suggested using wormwood in printing ink to stop rats eating printed paper.[16] One of Mascall's recipes is a true feast: a dram each of argentum sublimatum, regall and arsenic; twenty of the fattest figs; one ounce of hazelnuts; twelve walnuts; half a pound of wheatmeal; one pound and two ounces of hog's grease and a little honey.[17] Thomas Swaine, whose recipe for rat poison involves mixing a pound of arsenic with sugar and wheatmeal, stresses that it is important to wash one's hands after mixing rat poison and make sure that it is kept out of the reach of children. 'Desperate evils require desperate remedies.'[18]

The fact that the question of humane versus cruel methods of killing is raised suggests that in some contexts rats, despite their verminous status, have some consideration as sentient creatures. It is also a commonplace of ratcatchers in the past, and vermin control officers in recent years, to remark with admiration on the intelligence and adaptability of the rat. In his

A late 19th-century rat-trap.

A Finnish 'block' rat-trap.

'Surrey' rat-traps.

1908 survey of traps and methods of killing rats, Carl Prausnitz describes a trap patented in 1879. This was a narrow tunnel which caught the rat and gouged its body with sharp blades and prongs as it tried to escape. Prausnitz suggested that the advance of humane ideas since then meant that traps either killed animals instantly or caught them alive and that the tunnel trap was unacceptable.[19] Another method which had controversial application, especially around the turn of the twentieth century, was the use of virus preparations. These had first been tried out in Thessaly in 1892 against field-mice.[20] One was produced which involved salmonella; controversial, given the risk of poisoning humans. In 1908 the *British Medical Journal* called for its restriction. Defenders of salmonella as a rodenticide claimed that, given the bacteria was derived from the intestines of rats, it was pathogenic to that particular species.[21] However, outbreaks of possible poisoning in humans where the preparation had been used – reported in Liverpool and Japan – suggested otherwise. In 1967 the World Health Organization announced that salmonella should not be used in the killing of rats, but it continued to be used in Russia and Italy.[22] Rentokil, probably the most famous British pest control company, was founded in 1927 and then used a combination of salmonella and red squill. The latter was a poison derived from a lily (*Urginea maritima*) which had become popular in the later nineteenth century. Because it causes convulsions, it is now banned in the UK under the Animals (Cruel Poisons) Act of 1963. In 1939, the discovery of a chemical that produced haemorrhaging in cows that had

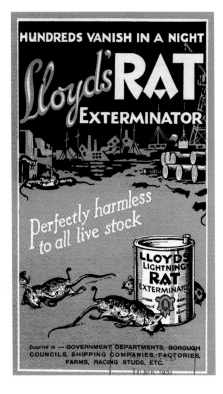

A Lloyd's rat exterminator leaflet of *c.* 1930.

eaten spoiled clover led, in the post-war years, to the development of the anti-coagulant poisons of which warfarin is one of the most famous.[23]

The variety of traps, poisons and other methods used against rats, plus the fact that rats have always been ineradicable suggests that rat killing is no more than, at best, an attempt to control a species. In the United States in 1936 the National Association of Exterminators and Fumigators voted to change the name 'exterminator' to 'pest control operator', in recognition of the need for realistic goals.[24] James Rodwell noted that the 1851 census revealed that there were 2,256 vermin killers in Britain and that the catches could be considerable. One

Paris sewermen with a box of rats, 1911.

The Royal Rat-catcher's sash, nowadays awarded annually to Rentokil's most efficient pest control manager.

ratcatcher in Suffolk, for instance, brought in 11,465 rats in a 21-week period while the main rat destroyers of London reckoned they killed about 8–9,000 per year.[25] In the early twentieth century, large estates like Sandringham in Norfolk produced a bag of some 20–30,000 a year, while for smaller estates 2–3,000 was not uncommon.[26]

Throughout the early twentieth century there was concern about the spread of rats. This intensified during the First World War when the reduced labour force meant a concomitant lapse in vermin control. The Incorporated Society for the Destruction of Vermin, founded in 1908, lobbied Parliament, set up a short-lived

A Danish rat tail cutter, a necessary tool for strict accounting.

journal and, as its first act, offered a ten-guinea prize for the best suggestion for putting rat skins to commercial use. A national rat killing competition was also proposed. This was an international movement. In France there was an Association Internationale pour la Destruction Rationnelle des Rats, and in 1907 in Denmark a centralized collecting and payment scheme was set up whereby all rats were to be brought to depots and a payment made on each one. Between July 1907 and 1908 this yielded 1,398,090 rats.[27] Although considerable efforts were made by various public bodies and companies in England between 1909 and 1916, by the end of the war there was deemed to be a serious vermin problem.[28] Despite the fact that in the House of Commons in 1919 the idea of presenting a debate on rats provoked 'considerable laughter', several sessions were devoted to a Rat Destruction Bill.[29] The intention was to make individuals responsible for the destruction of rats on their land. Failure to do so would bring punishment and compulsory official intervention. 'We have done a great deal of leaflets, pamphlets, and other propaganda, by utilising cinema, and in other ways to create what I may call an anti-rat atmosphere.'[30] The debate ultimately turned on whether this was an unnecessary imposition on the individual after the hardships of war. A choice between, as one speaker put it, a plague of rats or a plague of officials.

Although it is one of the features of the class of vermin that they are not eaten, rats are in fact consumed in many parts of the world. James Rodwell mentions rows of brown rats suspended by their tails in shops in Naples, like rows of onions. He also writes that the split, dried rats sold in China are delicate and sweet tasting.[31] In fact, many reports of eating rats are favourable. Jack Black, the ratcatcher immortalized by Mayhew, remarked that they were 'as moist as rabbits, and quite as nice'.[32] And a reporter for *National Geographic* remarked that eating rats in the Philippines deep fried in coconut oil 'had the pleasing gaminess of squirrel or rabbit'.[33] On the other hand, rats are the only animals that, for health reasons, SAS soldiers are not allowed to eat in the field.[34] A slightly more outlandish prohibition against eating rats in the eighteenth century was due to the fact that they were bad for your memory, which explained why cats did not have the attachment and fidelity of dogs. They simply forgot their owners due to a diet of rodents.[35] On his travels in Cornwall, the novelist Wilkie Collins mentions a rat hunt on Looe Island which resulted in the villagers feasting on their prey, 'ferociously *smothered in onions*' and laid out on clean china plates.[36] In fact, the rat has long been eaten in Asia, Latin America, and parts of Africa and Oceania and is a common hors-d'oeuvre.[37] Francis Buckland mentioned the sale of dried rats in China, 'their appearance being very much like that of the common English haddock'. These can be soaked and boiled, roasted or fried.[38] Peter Hessler's memorable recent account of a visit to two restaurants in southern China that

An Irula tribesman
holding up his
catch of rats.

serve rat – the Highest Ranking Wild Flavour Restaurant and
the New Eight Sceneries Wild Flavour Food City – attests to the
versatility of rat. He chooses the Simmered Mountain Rat with
Black Beans from a selection that includes steamed rat, rat
curry, and Mountain Rat Soup. You can choose your rat live
from the cages at the back of the restaurant before it is cooked.
Interestingly, eating rat in China is considered good for hair and
the prevention of baldness, a belief also mentioned by Gessner
in the seventeenth century.[39] In India the Irula, a nomadic people,
trap rats using the produce as food or for sale to crocodile farms
in Madras.[40] A recipe from nineteenth-century France gives
some sense of the evident versatility of rat meat by casseroling
rat in red wine. Perhaps more imaginative still is this one:

Narcisse Chaillou,
*The Rat-Seller
during the Siege of
Paris, c.* 1870–71,
oil on canvas.

40. - Siège de Paris (1870-71)
Au Marché St-Germain
Un Marchand de Chiens, Chats, Rats et Souris
A. J. H.

A print, c. 1871, showing a dog, cat, rat and mouse-merchant in the St-Germain market during the Siege of Paris.

. . . stuffed with a simple stuffing made of breadcrumbs, a sprinkling of sweet herbs, and a little pepper and salt, mixed with the liver and heart of a rat, and roasted for a few minutes in a hot oven, it proved to be a delicious dish not unlike snipe in flavour. Young rats may also be made into pies, if meat stock, consommé or a piece of beef be added to provide the gravy.[41]

Interactions between humans and rats are extensive, varied, and complicated. Rats have some sort of impact on almost every aspect of human life and culture, from cuisine to religion, from the arts to breeding, from science to sickness. They are reviled and abominated, admired and celebrated. Out of this highly fluid picture I have drawn attention to two features of rats in human history. The first is the way in which the rat becomes a key animal around the turn of the twentieth century in the West and epitomises the interaction between technology and nature, as well as new configurations of animals in the twentieth century. Because the rat is so bound up with ideas of mass and number it seems to be a totemic animal for the modern world. The second feature is the human love/hate relationship with the rat. The rat comes to be described by many as the most reviled animal, especially from the seventeenth and eighteenth centuries onwards, and yet at the same time remains central to human preoccupations. Ultimately, rat bodies are both fluid and boundary breaking. They flood over and gnaw through borders real and imagined. They have a dark vitality that, despite all the control and killing, we do not overcome.

Engraving of a 'rat-king' found, still alive, in Erfurt, Germany, in 1772.

Timeline of the Rat

230–190 mya	55 mya	37–24 mya	*c.* 14mya	3,500 BC
Rodent-like reptiles	Beginning of the order of rodents	Appearance of myomorphs	Divergence of rats and mice	Very early archaeological remains of rats in Sardinia

1346	1551	1565	1621
The Black Death begins	Publication begins of Conrad Gessner's *Historia Animalium* containing an encyclopaedic account of the rat	Rats reach Florida. By the mid-16th century they have reached the Pacific Coast of North America	First recorded rat dissection by Theophilus Müller and Johannes Farber

1894	1900	1901	1906	1909
Outbreak of bubonic plague in Hong Kong; Yersin and Roux prove that bubonic plague is an illness of the rat. In 1898 Simond proves that bubonic plague is spread by rat fleas	Plague outbreak in Glasgow	First appearance of rats in an animal show in England	Standardized laboratory rats begin to be produced at the Wistar Institute, Philadelphia	Freud's 'Rat Man' Case is published

1,600–1,500 BC	AD 100–200	AD 541	c. 1000
Archaeological remains of rats found in Iraq and Egypt	Rats spread along the Rhine and Rhone river networks and into Britain	The first plague pandemic spreads from Egypt to Europe and Asia Minor	The word *raet* appears in Aelfric's *Glossary*

early 1700s	1803	1830	1858
Arrival of the brown rat in Britain. By the 1760s it has reached British America	First suggested scientific division of *Rattus* as a separate creature from mice	Waterhouse divides rodents into 2 classes: rabbits and all the others. The first use of 'rodent' in English occurs in the 1830s	Publication of James Rodwell's *The Rat: its history and destructive character with numerous anecdotes*

1910–11	1931	1974	2003	2004
Plague-bearing rats found in Suffolk, England	Harlan Sprague-Dawley Inc. founded, producing rats on a commercial basis	First Rat Olympics held at Nebraska Wesleyan University	Inception of World Rat Day, 4 April. In the same year the first cloned rat is produced, named Ralph	Genome map published for *Rattus norvegicus*

A 1650s tableau that includes a decomposing body being eaten by rats.

Appendix:
A Legend of the Inquisition (1890)

In the darkness of the dolorous time,
When simple faith was the only crime,
And the earth had lost its Gospel chime,
There was done a deed in Spain –
A deed, though generations old,
At which the very blood runs cold,
And the heart turns sick with pain.

In the time, when the Inquisition lay,
Like a thunder cloud upon the day,
And the iron grip of its grim sway
Into men's hearts had grown,
There was done this deed of bitter shame
On a woman fair of noble name,
Who called her will her own.

When she dared to love her husband best
To be faithful still though sorely prest
By the priests, who, while she sins confest,
To worse sins tried to lure;
They denounced her, they denounced her lord,
Because she feared not rack or sword,
And kept her purpose pure.

They were dragged before that court so fell,
Which was but the upper court of hell;
For they loved their honour all too well,
More than their living breath;
And the sentence of their secret doom,
Was recorded in the judgment gloom,
And the sentence it was death.

Then his wife was slain before his face,
Because she scorned to be so base,
As to yield to them her spotless grace,
What makes a matron strong;
And before his staring maddened eyes,
And beneath the veiled and silent skies,
Was done this damnéd wrong.

But first in the black defiling dust,
They wreaked on her all their hellish lust,
Though they could not break her woman's trust,
In the great God of love;
Though they laid her outraged body low,
Yet the angels came in the sunset glow,
And they took her soul above.

Then they bound the live man to the dead,
And they bound them fast from foot to head,
And they spurned him with their cruel tread,
As a master spurns the slave;
And they left him in that ghastly life,
The husband with his butchered wife,
In the darkness of the grave.

They were wedded in a marriage strange,
And stern as the tomb that knows not change,
When the thought alone can freely range,
And madness is the thought;
They were wedded in that funeral place,
And they mingled in that last embrace,
That the hand of hell had wrought.
And the white lips lay upon his own,
But the spirit warm had from them flown,
And they spoke of mysteries unknown,
But they breathed no tender breath;
And their message he might never guess,
In the silence of that cold caress,
Which was the kiss of death.

And he listened as his heart beat on,
Till the last low lingering step was gone,
And the last dim lantern no more shone,
Till the light *within* went out;
And he looked as dying souls for day,
Till the last pale shadow passed away,
With the distant ribald shout.

And he was alone with his heart and God,
Alone like a man in the burial sod,
And the ghostly stillness on him trod,
Like the weight of the coffin lead;
And his thoughts ran high in a raging flood,

As he lay in the horror and the blood,
Alone with his precious dead.
For the key was turned and the bolts were shot,
And for him had fallen the changeless lot,
And the massive door would open not,
Till his pulse had ceased to beat;
And he cried for mercy, and the walls
Re-echoed his despairing calls,
From out their stony seat.

But he cried in vain from his iron cage,
And the moment seemed an endless age,
And the cell the universe's stage,
And his breast a battle ground;
There was night without in the rayless gloom,
There was night within in the dreadful doom,
That his soul with darkness bound.

And he felt the warm blood slowly drip,
From the corpse and each dumb crimson lip,
And each drop falling seemed to slip
Into his heart's own tide;
And the hours went by, and there he lay,
In the tomb that slew, and did not slay,
With the dead thing at his side.

But, hark! a sound as of friendly feet,
Mustering many and mustering fleet;
If the message were God's, the voice were sweet,
For it would release the slave;
They are coming and coming, an army strong;
He has waited late, he has waited long,
In the grip of that living grave.

They will break his bonds, they will set him free,
The light will arise and the shadows flee,
And the blinded eyes again shall see
The woman he loved so well;
And the dreadful dream in which he lies,
It will pass like a thunder-cloud from the skies,
Or the throb of a funeral bell.

There is help for the helpless soul at last,
There is hope for the hopeless, fear is past,
And the burdened breast its cares can cast
On the Lord who bids him come;
There is rest for the restless grinding pains,
Remembrance of forgotten chains,
And for the weary home.

But what do they mean? For the sounds are
    strange.
Has his mind, in its maddened wandering
    range –
Has his mind gone through some awful change,
And mocked his brain with din?
Is the noise outside in the ghostly space?
Or is fancy but its dwelling-place,
And is its seat within?

Oh, is it the wind from his mountain moor,
Chittering, chattering,
Pittering, pattering,
Over the breadth of the bloody floor,
Out of the walls and under the door,
Hurrying, scurrying,
Flurrying, worrying –
Has the wind swept down to visit the poor?

Is it lapsing of raindrops on the leaves,
Tinkling and twinkling,
Calling and falling,
Fretting the edge of familiar eaves,
Flying in spray from the arméd sheaves,
Dripping and dropping,
Chipping and chopping
The pebbles to which the dust still cleaves?

Is he dreaming? Or are they waves that beat,
Leaping and lisping,
Creeping and crisping,
Shy in the shadow and bold in the heat,
Up to the foot of the castled seat,
Nearer and nearer,
Clearer and clearer,
Dancing to light from their dim retreat?

Are they feet of his children upon the mats,
Sliding and gliding,
Hiding and chiding,
That come flitting across the marble flats? –
Or are they the wings of the vampire bats,
Rustling and bustling,
Hustling and justling? –
Or are they – Oh, are they the damnéd rats?

At the ghastly thought, his heart stood still
And he heard afar the laughing rill,
As it hastened down his native hill,
In its bright enriching track;
He saw it all in a moment's time,
And the music of its happy chime,
Brought his whole history back.

It all came back, with his childhood's toys,
And the mother's smile that caught her boy's,
And the splendour of his springtide joys,
And the service of the sword;
He knelt once more by his Inez' side,
When his love became a soldier's bride,
And he gave her to the Lord.
And then as the dreadful truth came nigh,
His breast was torn with a tempest sigh,
And his heart beat quick and his heart beat high,
Like a steed that longs to start;
And face to face with the frightful death,
He clenched his teeth and he held his breath,
To play a conqueror's part.

And lo! in a kind of trancèd daze,
Through the horror of the battle haze,
He saw the ranks in their rhythmic maze,
And many a noble Don;
He saw the red masses backward reel,
From a moving wall of flashing steal,
That still kept rolling on.

Then he felt the rats in their legions steal,
To the feasting of that funeral meal,
On the face his hands would fain conceal,
Were they not in fetters tied;
And they peeled the precious tender flesh,
Grew tired, and the began afresh,
And were yet unsatisfied.

And they tore her tresses, shred by shred,
As the bloom of a glorious flower is shed;
But they lingered on the lovely red,
Where the red rose had been;
And God, in his mercy, veiled the night
Of the living man in dusky night,
From the things he might have seen.

For they crept and crawled, a hideous rout,
Laid bare the skull, and in and out
They swarmed, and revelled all about,
To find some feast to suit;
They gnawed and nibbled, rent the skin
To suck the sweetness from within,
As one might rend a fruit.

They fought and frolicked o'er their prey,
And none were better fed than they;
Till his jet black hair grew stiff and grey,
And his mind began to rave;
And he heard his teeth at work on her
He loved, like the pick of the grave-digger
Digging his own dark grave.
And the cruel greedy crunching sound
Went on, in its dull and ceaseless round,
As the busy fangs were sharper ground
On the once so lovely form;
And outside the walls of that dismal deep,
There came echoes as from the land of sleep –
Were they guns, or a gathering storm?

And he listened and listened, in breathless need;
But the feasting rats, they took no heed,
As they stript the frame in ravenous greed
Of the features that made it fair;
And when they were full, with emulous pace
Fresh troops poured in to take their place,
In the reeking fetid air.

And still they came in their hungry hosts,
They squeaked and moaned like gibbering
   ghosts,
And still drove in the outward posts
Of the army on the field;
They fought with frantic tooth and nail
For the dainty food, ere it should fail,
That none would lightly yield.

And his straining face was ashen gray,
As he cried to God for breaking day;
And the rats they gnawed and gnawed alway,
Till his starting eyes grew dim;
But the sun would rise and the sun would set,
And the mother might her child forget,
Yet nought would shine on him.

In the blackness of that bloody strife,
On the shapeless thing that was his wife,
It seemed each rent was the butcher's knife,
And was driven into his frame;
It seemed as if for him they fought,
On him the devilry was wrought
That had no Christian name.

Each tap of the feet that darkness hid,
As a rat was gorged and downward slid,
Was the hammer's tap on the coffin lid,
From a hand that would not spare;
And the work went on, and the work went fast,
Till the awful meal was done at last,
And they picked the body bare.

And now was a pause in the dreadful deed,
While fresh rats gathered still to feed,
And still they came in their cursèd speed,
And they all had to be fed . . .
But then they turned to the living man,
And on him once more fresh hosts began,
While they tore him shred by shred.

And the lean grew fat and the fat grew more,
As they revelled in human flesh and gore,
And they gnawed and nibbled, sucked and tore,
And ground as the millstones grind;
For they plucked the meat to the very bone,
As a dainty girl, though she has but one,
From the apple sheds its rind.

And they gouged his eyes and gauged his lips,
They clove to the cheeks with relentless grips,
And tasted his throat with greedy sips,
In their hunger great and grim;
And they rent him piecemeal, till the bands
They rattled upon his fleshless hands,
And they fastened on every limb.

As he heard the grating rasping strain,
He laughed like a marked undying Cain,
And he laughed till the walls they laughed again,
And the rats one moment stopped;
For it seemed to him, as he maddened lay,
They were feasting on something far away,
That the battle had somewhere dropped.

He felt no pain in the cutting pangs,
And there was no edge to the cruel fangs,
For his sense was dead as the life that hangs
Over the pit of death;
Though he knew the damnèd rats were there,
And rats and rats were everywhere,
And he drank their short sharp breath.

Though he heard them picking, picking still,
And each one worked its savage will,
And each one ate its ghastly fill,
Till they could eat no more;
Though he saw the branding on his brain,
Yet never he felt a pulse of pain,
As he felt for her before.

And a fire within him seemed to burn,
As the embers in the funeral urn,
While fresh rats quarreled for their turn,
For the flesh of man is sweet;
And they had starved and waited long,
They were mad for food and fresh and strong,
And the famine winged their feet.

But again he heard that volleying sound,
That like a tempest wrapped him round –
Was it overhead or underground?
Or within his reeling mind?
And with those echoing thunder tones,
The teeth went on like chattering stones,
That cannot choose but grind.

It nearer drew and yet more near,
It clearer came and yet more clear,
Like a message to the mournful ear
Of the soul that fortune shuns;
And he strained till his ribs began to start,
For he knew it in his soldier's heart –
It was the sound of guns.

And onward still the tumult came,
With the clash of swords and the glare of flame,
Till it rolled unto those walls of shame,
And it thundered at the door;
And the rats they fled from that slaughter room,
And he heard them scattering through the
  gloom,
And plashing over the floor.

A wonderment filled his soul! And then,
There trod into his troubled ken
The heavy tramp of armèd men,
With the clanking of the sword;
And it seemed to his poor clouded brain,
As if the old life had dawned again,
And he of himself was lord.

Then the tide swept in, till it reached the cell,
And the bars before its billows fell,
As the earthquake rends its earthen shell,
And vengeance flashed its light;
But the men who would rather die than yield,
And were blood-stained from the battle field,
Stood awestruck at the sight.

Lo, there was the dead to the living bound,
And the fleshless jaws they mumbled sound,
While the eyeless sockets stared around,
And the clean-picked head stood white;
For the thing half-eaten still lived on,
And jabbered to the skeleton,
And the fingers strove to write.

And there in the light of that judgment day,
In a resurrection cold and gray,
By the dead and the dying the live rats lay
So gorged that they could not fly;
And there was the man who would not sell
His soul, and the woman who loved too well
Her honour and purity.

The stones were strewn with knots of hair,
And bloody rags, that once were fair;
And bloody steps ran down the stair,
With more that did not show;
The air was thick with bloody fume,
And the red torch shone but to illume
The redder pools below.
And the rugged face turned sad and soft,
While the vow of vengeance trembled oft,
And many a sword was held aloft
By many a strong right hand;
And the hardened soldiers turned away

From the woe no mortal could allay,
As it passed to the silent land.

Then a cry of horror and of hate
The prison shook to its utmost gate,
When they measured all the accurséd fate
Of the grimly-wedded twain;
And they hunted far and hunted wide,
For the fiends who had killed a woman's pride,
And a man had doubly slain.

Till they dragged them from their holes of shade,
At the point of the pursuing blade,
To every torture they had made,
And every hellish doom;
To see the future grow more black,
To lie on the more dreadful rack
Of memory's torture-room.

And they chained the murderers cheek by jowl,
In the reverend cassock and the cowl,
And laid them with their dying howl,
In the darkness with the bats;
With their gimcracks and their Devil's tricks,
Their crosses and their candlesticks,
They left them to the rats.

FREDERICK WILLIAM ORDE WARD (1843–1922)

References

INTRODUCTION

1 Letter to Frank Belknap Long, 8 November 1923. S. T. Joshi and David E. Schultz (eds), *Lord of a Visible World: An Autobiography in Letters* (Athens, OH, 2000), pp. 122–3. The narrator's cat in 'The Rats in the Walls' is called Nigger-Man.

2 T. S. Eliot, 'Burbank with a Baedeker: Bleistein with a Cigar', *Collected Poems, 1909–1935* (London, 1954), p. 41. The link between rats and Jews has often been made in an anti-Semitic context. For instance, the Nazi propaganda film *Die Ewige Jude* likened the spread of rats across the world to the wandering of Jews; Boria Sax, *Animals in the Third Reich: Pets, Scapegoats and the Holocaust* (New York, 2000), p. 159.

3 H. P. Lovecraft, 'The Rats in the Walls', in *The Call of Cthulhu and Other Weird Stories* (Harmondsworth, 1999), pp. 89–108.

4 James Rodwell, *The Rat: Its History and Destructive Character with Numerous Anecdotes* (London, 1858).

5 On the relationship between the physical and symbolic aspects of horror, see Julia Kristeva, *Powers of Horror* (New York, 1982), especially relevant comments on pp. 65–72.

6 Hans Zinsser, *Rats, Lice and History* (Harmondsworth, 2000), pp. 208–9.

7 Robert Sullivan, *Rats: Observations on the History and Habitat of the City's Most Unwanted Inhabitants* (New York, 2004), p. 2.

1 NATURAL HISTORY

1 David Alderton, *Rodents of the World* (London, 1999), p. 9; Peter Hanney, *Rodents: Their Lives and Habitats* (Newton Abbott, 1975), pp. 13, 33.

2 R. Adkins et al., 'Molecular Phylogeny and Divergence Time Estimates for Major Rodent Groups: Evidence from Multiple Genes', *Molecular Biology and Evolution*, XVIII (2001), pp. 771–7.

3 Anna D'Erchia et al., 'The Guinea Pig Is Not a Rodent', *Nature*, 381 (1996), p. 597.

4 Edwin Colbert, Michael Morales and Eli Minkoff, *Colbert's Evolution of Vertebrates* (5th edn, New York, 2001), p. 363.

5 Edward R. Alston, 'On the Classification of the Order', *Proceedings of the Zoological Society of London* (1876), p. 61.

6 Hanney, *Rodents*, p. 246.

7 J. Michaux et al., 'Evolutionary History of the Most Speciose Mammals: Molecular Phylogeny Of Muroid Rodents', *Molecular Biology and Evolution*, XVIII (2001), pp. 2017–31.

8 D. R. Rosevear, *The Rodents of West Africa* (London, 1969), pp. 246–7: 'In many parts of the world there are rodents commonly called rats, such as South American spiny rats, or the cane rats, and naked mole rats of Africa, although they belong to a different suborder from *Rattus* itself.'

9 Albert Wood, 'The Early Tertiary Rodents of the Family *Paramyidae*', *Transactions of the American Philosophical Society*, LII (1962), pp. 244–5. The most primitive type of enamel in mammalian teeth is radial, in which all the prisms run parallel and radially towards the outer surface. In most mammals with gliriform incisors the enamel is much more differentiated and thus stronger. W. von Koenigswald, 'Evolutionary Trends in the Enamel of Rodent Incisors', in W. P. Luckett and J. L. Hardenberger, eds, *Evolutionary Relationships among Rodents: A Multidisciplinary Analysis* (London, 1985), p. 405.

10 Thomas Martin, 'Early Rodent Incisor Enamel Evolution: Phylogenetic Implications', *Journal of Mammalian Evolution*, 1 (1993), pp. 227–54.

11 Hanney, *Rodents*, p. 21.

12 R.J.G. Savage and M. R. Long, *Mammal Evolution: An Illustrated Guide* (London, 1986), p. 116.

13 Rodents exhibit rates of amino acid replacement twice that of observed for non-rodents, Adkins et al., 'Molecular Phylogeny'.

14 J. L. Hardenberger, 'The Order *Rodentia*: Major Questions on their Evolutionary Origin, Relationships, and Suprafamilial Systematics', in *Evolutionary Relationships* ed. Luckett and Hardenberger, p. 17.

15 Li Chuan-Kuei et al., 'The Origin of Rodents and Lagomorphs', *Current*

Mammology, I (1987), p. 98.

16 Savage and Long, *Mammal Evolution*, p. 113.

17 Ibid., pp. 116–24.

18 Alderton, *Rodents of the World*, pp. 138–44.

19 Philip Armitage, 'Unwelcome Companions: Ancient Rats Reviewed', *Antiquity*, LXVIII (1994), p. 238; S. Coram-Mekkey, 'Peste et rat: un couple indissociable', *Moyen Age*, CIII (1977), p. 148.

20 F. Audoin-Rouzeau and J.-D. Vigne, 'La colonisation de l'Europe par le rat noir (*Rattus rattus*)', *Revue de Paléobiologie*, XIII (1994), p. 126.

21 Tosihide Yoshida, *Cytogenetics of the Black Rat: Karyotype Evolution and Species Differentiation* (Tokyo, 1980). He confirms the point that rodents show more frequent chromosome evolution than other mammals. Incidentally, the word commensal distinguishes the rat from a true parasite, meaning literally 'sharing a table with'. Unlike a parasite, the rat does not live off, or in, the body of its host.

22 S. A. Barnett, *The Story of Rats* (Crows Nest, NSW, 2001), p. 19.

23 See Audoin-Rouzeau and Vigne, 'La colonisation de l'Europe', for a list of the archaeological evidence; also Coram-Mekkey, 'Peste et rat', p. 143. For a thesis about rats in Israel with a date of 9,500–7,500 BC, see E. Tchernov, 'Commensal Animals and Human Sedentism in the Middle East', in *Animals and Archaeology 3: Early Herders and their Flocks*, ed. Juliet Clutton-Brock and Caroline Grigson, BAR International Series 202 (Oxford, 1984), p. 92.

24 James Rackham, '*Rattus rattus*: The Introduction of the Black Rat into Britain', *Antiquity*, LIII (1979), pp. 112–20; Philip Armitage, Barbara West and Ken Steedman, 'New Evidence of the Black Rat in London', *London Archaeologist*, IV (1984), pp. 375–83.

25 Armitage, 'Unwelcome Companions', p. 234.

26 T. P. O'Connor, 'Pets and Pests in Roman and Medieval Britain', *Mammal Review*, XXII (1992), p. 108.

27 Philip Armitage, 'Commensal Rats in the New World, 1492–1992', *Biologist*, XL (1993), pp. 175–7.

28 G. I. Twigg, 'The Black Rat *Rattus rattus* in the United Kingdom in 1989', *Mammal Review*, XXII (1992), pp. 33–42. Twigg notes that global warming and the opening of the Channel Tunnel may favour a revival in the fortunes of the black rat.

2 NATURAL HISTORIANS AND THE RAT

1 Conrad Gessner, *Historiae Animalium Liber Primus De Quadrupedipus Viviparis* (Cambieriano, 1603), p. 731.

2 Edward Topsell, *The Historie of the Four-footed Beasts* (London, 1607), p. 519. He also notes the appearance of white rats in Germany.

3 C. G. Bourdon de Sigrais, *Histoire des Rats* (Ratopolis [Paris], 1738), p. 130.

4 Peter Stallybrass and Allon White, *The Politics and Poetics of Transgression* (London, 1986), p. 143.

5 Mary Fissell, 'Imagining Vermin in Early Modern England', *History Workshop Journal*, XLVII (1999), p. 23.

6 Philippus Camerarius, *The Living Librarie; or, Meditations and Observations Historical, Natvral, Moral, Political, and Poetical* (London, 1621), p. 26.

7 Peter Pallas, *Novae species quadrupedum e Glirium Ordine* (Erlangae, 1778), p. 92.

8 Thomas Bewick, *A Description of above 300 Animals* (2nd edn, Alnwick, 1820), p. 40.

9 Thomas Pennant, *British Zoology* (London, 1768–70), vol. I, pp. 98–100.

10 There are some parallels between this and the culturally favoured status of the red squirrel over the grey in the twentieth century; see Hilda Kean, 'Imagining Rabbits and Squirrels in the English Countryside', *Society and Animals*, IX (2001), pp. 163–75.

11 Julia Blackburn, *Charles Waterton, 1782–1865: Conservationist and Naturalist* (London, 1997), p. 5.

12 Charles Waterton, *Essays on Natural History, Chiefly Ornithology* (London, 1838), pp. 211–12.

13 Blackburn, *Charles Waterton*, p. 6. 'He saw himself as a black rat marooned on the safe island of his house and his park, while all around him, beyond this boundary, the English landscape was filled with Hanoverians of one sort or another.'

14 Charles Waterton, *Essays on Natural History, Chiefly Ornithology* (London, 1844), p. 17.

15 Waterton, *Essays* (1838), p. 212.

16 John Berkenhout, *Synopsis of the Natural History of Great Britain and Ireland* (London, 1795), vol. I, p. 5. For observations on the disappearance of the black rat in the eighteenth and nineteenth centuries, see Gerald

Barrett-Hamilton and Martin A. C. Hinton, *A History of British Mammals* (London, 1916), part XIX, p. 584.

17 J. E. Harting, *Essays on Sport and Natural History* (London, 1883), p. 156.

18 M. le Comte de Buffon, *Histoire naturelle, generale et particuliere: quadrupedes tome II* (Paris: 1781), p. 271.

19 Ibid., p. 274.

20 Baron Cuvier, *La Règne animal distribué d'après son organisation, pour servir de base à l'histoire naturelle des animaux* (Paris, 1829), vol. I, p. 200. On the way in which patterns in teeth enamel are used to class rodents, see G. R. Waterhouse, *A Natural History of Mammalia* (London, 1846–8), vol. II, pp. 2–4.

21 Thomas Bewick, *A General History of Quadrupeds* (Newcastle upon Tyne, 1790), p. 355.

22 Charles Fothergill, *An Essay on the Philosophy, Study and Use of Natural History* (London, 1813), p. 137.

23 Ibid., p. 139.

24 Francis T. Buckland, *Curiosities of Natural History* (London, 1857), p. 70.

25 Quoted in Barrett-Hamilton and Hinton, *A History*, p. 625.

26 William I. Miller, *The Anatomy of Disgust* (Cambridge, MA, 1997), pp. 168–70. Miller writes with regard to Stallybrass and White that the rat is marginal no matter what the operative scheme, 'whether in times with underground sewers or in times without them. The rat, like faeces, seems to be somewhat independent of structure', p. 276n.

27 William Mcgillivray, *British Quadrupeds* (Edinburgh, 1843), p. 238.

28 Ibid., p. 244.

29 J. G. Millais, *The Mammals of Great Britain and Ireland*, 3 vols (London, 1904–6), vol. II, p. 221.

30 Ibid., pp. 223–4.

31 Ibid., p. 232.

32 A. P. Meehan, *Rats and Mice: Their Biology and Control* (East Grinstead, 1984), p. 19.

33 Robert Sullivan, *Rats: Observations on the History and Habitat of the City's Most Unwanted Inhabitants* (New York, 2004), pp. 15ff.

34 D. Chitty and H. N. Southern (eds), *Control of Rats and Mice*, 3 vols (Oxford, 1954).

3 RAT REPRESENTATIONS

1 George Cansdale, *Animals of Bible Lands* (Exeter, 1970), p. 39.

2 Otto Neustatter, 'Mice in Plague Pictures', *Journal of the Walters Art Gallery*, IV (1941), pp. 105–8. Neustatter noted a wax relief by the seventeenth-century artist Gaetano Zumbo in which the decomposing bodies of plague victims in a common grave are preyed upon by rats. Zumbo's 'La Vanita della Gloria umana' was likened to the 'Melancoria' created by Vasari for Michelangelo's tomb. A goddess looks upon decaying human bodies whose rotting flesh is eaten by rats and snakes.

3 Neustatter, 'Mice in Plague Pictures', p. 109.

4 P. J. Dillon and E. L. Jones, 'Trevor Falla's Vermin Transcripts for Devon', *Devon Historian*, XXXIII (1986), pp. 15–19; T. N. Brushfield, 'On the Destruction of "Vermin" in Rural Parishes', *Report and Transactions of the Devonshire Association for the Advancement of Science, Literature and Art*, XXIX (1897), pp. 291–349.

5 Hans Zinsser, *Rats, Lice and History* (London, 1985), p. 192.

6 Aelian, *On the Characteristics of Animals*, VI, 41.

7 Latin *mus* can refer to mouse, rat, sable, marten and ermine. I have used the term rat for this section for simplicity, with the caveat that the word may mean another kind of rodent in the original Greek or Latin.

8 Aristotle, *History of Animals*, 581a3–6.

9 Aelian, *Characteristics*, XVII, 17.

10 Plutarch, *Natural Phenomena*, III, 912. Pliny reproduces much of this and remarks that rats / mice are so fertile that they impregnate each other by licking; *Natural History*, X, 85.

11 Pliny, *Natural History*, X, 85.

12 Strabo, *Geography*, 13.1.47–8; Aelian, *Characteristics*, XII, 5.

13 Herodotus, *Histories*, II, 141. See also the story of the gift of the rat to Darius in IV, 131ff.

14 Raymond Crawfurd, *Plague and Pestilence in Literature and Art* (Oxford, 1914), p. 17.

15 Pliny, *Natural History*, VIII, 82.

16 Stith Thompson, *Motif Index of Folk Literature*, 6 vols (revd edn, Copenhagen, 1955–8).

17 Verrier Elwin, *Tribal Myths of Orissa* (Bombay, 1954), p. 682.

18 Charles Swynnerton, *Indian Nights' Entertainment* (London, 1892), pp. 269–70.

19 Y. Krishan, *Ganesa: Unravelling an Enigma* (Delhi, 1999), p. 50. Alice Getty sees the rat as symbolizing night, *Ganesa: A Monograph on the Elephant-faced God* (Oxford, 1936), p. 1.

20 Wendy O'Flaherty, *Hindu Myths* (Harmondsworth, 1975), p. 269.

21 Ryan Grube, 'Daikoku', www.uwec.edu/philrel/shimbutsudo/daikoku.html (November 2004).

22 Catherine M. Goguel, '*La Batrachomyomachie*, un thème rare: du rat de la fable au rat des savants', in *L'Illustration: essais d'iconographie*, ed. M. T. Caracciolo and S. Le Men (Klincksieck, 1999), p. 252.

23 La Fontaine, *Fables* (Tours, 1877), pp. 378–80.

24 Roger L'Estrange, *Fables of Aesop . . .* (London, 1692), p. 79.

25 Elvin, *Orissa*, p. 683.

26 Verrier Elwin, *Myths of Middle India* (Bombay, 1949), p. 279.

27 Elwin, *Orissa*, pp. 404–5.

28 Aelian, *Characteristics*, XII, 10.

29 Jacques Berchtold, *Des Rats et ratières: anamorphoses d'un champ métaphorique de saint Augustin à Jean Racine* (Geneva, 1992), pp. 101–2, 113–14.

30 For other more recent examples of rats and sexuality, see George Groddeck, *The Book of the It* (London, 1961), p. 214. Bataille links sex to the idea of the rat, 'nakedness is the only death and the tenderest kisses have an after-taste of rat'. See G. Bataille, *The Impossible: A Story of Rats* (San Francisco, 1991), p. 81; see also pp. 53–4. Antonin Artaud likewise uses the figure of the abject rat, along with sexuality and cannibalism, in his targeting of religion: J. Derrida and P. Thevenin, *The Secret Art of Antonin Artaud* (Cambridge, MA, 1998), p. 154.

31 Barbara Rosen (ed.), *Witchcraft* (London, 1969), p. 381.

32 Martha Beckwith, *Hawaiian Mythology* (Honolulu, 1970), pp. 424–5

33 Edward W. Gifford, 'Tongan Myths and Tales', *Bernice P. Bishop Museum Bulletin (Honolulu)*, VIII (1924), pp. 206–7.

34 Iona Opie and Moira Tatem, *A Dictionary of Superstitions* (Oxford, 1989), p. 322. It is noted that in East Anglia many people will not use the word rat but will say something in its place.

35 E. Bradford and M. A. Bradford, *Encyclopaedia of Superstitions* (London,

1969), pp. 280–81.

36 Alasdair MacGregor, 'The Pied Piper', *Folk-Lore*, LXVI (1955), p. 432. Another rat charmer who used a whistle 'which seems to have a hypnotic effect on rats, causing them to crawl to him' is described in Charles Thomas, 'Present Day Charmers in Cornwall', *Folk-Lore*, LXIV (1953), p. 304.

37 Pliny, *Natural History*, X, 85.

38 Silvanus Thompson, *The Pied Piper of Hamelin* (London, 1905), p. 26. Thompson notes a number of possible dates for the Hamelin episode, including the late twelfth century, and the idea that it is an allegory for the Children's Crusade of 1211. It has also been claimed that the story symbolizes the confusion of tongues and the dispersion of builders after the Tower of Babel: Abraham Elder, *Tales and Legends of the Isle of Wight* (2nd edn, London, 1843), p. 136. Note also the Rat-Wife in Ibsen's *Little Eyolf* (1894) who goes round freeing the countryside of rats by charming them into the sea.

39 Berchtold, *Rats et ratières*, p. 16.

40 Ibid., p. 89.

41 Sabine Baring-Gould, *Curious Myths of the Middle Ages* (London, 1872), p. 463.

42 Ibid., p. 460.

43 W. Deonna, 'La «boule aux rats» et le monde trompeur', *Revue Archaéologique*, LI–LII (1958), pp. 51–75.

44 See Robert Southey's poem 'God's Judgement on a Wicked Bishop', 'And now they pick the Bishop's bones; / They gnaw'd the flesh from every limb, / For they were sent to do judgement on him.'

45 M. K. Booker, 'The Rats of God: Joyce, Pynchon, Beckett and the Carnivalisation of Religion', *Pynchon Notes*, 24–25 (1989), p. 21. Thus in Beckett's *Watt*, the characters Sam and Watt feed rats to each other, remarking that on such occasions they felt 'nearest to God'.

46 Christopher Herbert, 'Rat Worship and Taboo in Mayhew's London', *Representations*, XXIII (1988), p. 19.

47 Ibid., p. 15. In a more recent article Herbert discusses the Victorian idea that in primitive taboo sanctity and uncleanness were indistinguishable. Taboo things also have a 'deadly energy', or holiness, that is conceived as infectious, propagating itself by physical contact; C. Herbert, 'Vampire Religion', *Representations*, LXXIX (2002), p. 103.

48 There are numerous examples in fiction of the poor being likened to rats. See, for instance, Patrick Macgill, *The Rat-Pit* (London, 1915), p. v; Bram Stoker, 'The Burial of the Rats', in *The Bram Stoker Bedside Companion* (London, 1974), p. 70.

49 Hugh Sykes Davis, *The Papers of Andrew Melmoth* (London, 1960), p. 209. Likewise, in Thomas Pynchon's novel *V* (1963), a priest goes into the New York sewers to preach to rats and convert them to Christianity because he believes that they will rule the world when civilization ends. Other versions of this appear in fantasy novels such as Mary Gentle's *Rats and Gargoyles* (London, 1990), in which rats are masters over humans, many of the latter hiding in the sewers. The notion that radioactivity will speed up the evolution of rats to the detriment of humans is a frequent motif, appearing in Sykes Davis but also in horror stories like James Herbert's *The Rats*.

50 Davies, *The Papers*, p. 166.

51 C. G. Bourdon de Sigrais, *Histoire des Rats* (Ratopolis [Paris], 1738), pp. 13–4, 19–21. Amusingly, this work is dedicated to rats, notable bibliophages, so that it won't be eaten since the rat's interest in its own glory should overcome its habitual avidity.

52 C. Fitzgibbon, *The Rat Report* (London, 1980), p. 14.

53 George Orwell, *1984* (London, 2003), p. 244.

54 Ibid., pp. 328–9.

55 Quoted in Leonard Shengold, *Soul Murder: The Effects of Childhood Abuse and Deprivation* (New Haven, 1989), p. 81.

56 Albert Camus, *The Plague* (London, 2001), p. 54.

57 Seamus Heaney, *Death of a Naturalist* (London, 1991), pp. 6–7.

58 Ted Hughes, *Collected Animal Poems* (London, 1995), pp. 24–6.

59 Alan Sillitoe, *Collected Poems* (London, 1993), p. 23.

60 Rats appear in the writings of the Vietnam War where they often seem as much to be pitied as eradicated. For examples see Kurt Dittmar, 'Of Rats and Soldiers: Reflections on the Topos of Modern War Literature', *Amerikastudien*, xxxviii (1993), pp. 625–37.

61 R. van Emden (ed.), *Tickled to Death to Go: Memoirs of a Cavalryman in the First World War* (Staplehurst, Kent, 1996), pp. 134–5. 'There was more gas at night. It should thin out the rats, filthy pests', Captain J. C. Dunn, *The War the Infantry Knew, 1914–1919* (London, 2001), p. 198.

62 David Jones, *In Parenthesis* (London, 1963), p. 54.

63 *The Collected Poems of Isaac Rosenberg*, ed. G. Bottomley and Denys Harding (London, 1977), p. 73.

64 Alison McMahan, *Alice Guy Blaché: Lost Visionary of the Cinema* (New York, 2003), p. 167.

65 Maarten't Hart, 'Rats', *Granta*, 86 (2004), p. 77.

66 S. S. Prawer, *Nosferatu – Phantom der Nacht* (London, 2004), pp. 22, 47.

67 Kier La Janisse, 'Willard, the New Rat Pack', *Fangoria*, April 2003, pp. 24–8.

4 THE 'HERO OF SCIENCE'

1 Robert Boyle, *The Works of the Honourable Robert Boyle* (London, 1744), vol. I, pp. 63–4.

2 *The Times*, 24 July 1837, p. 7.

3 J. R. Lindsey, 'Historical Foundations', *The Laboratory Rat*, ed. H. J. Baker, J. R. Lindsey and S. H. Weisbroth (London, 1979), pp. 2–36. This is one of the most useful summary accounts of the history of the laboratory rat. The history of rats in science has been well documented in outline, especially from the late nineteenth century onwards, but requires more detailed study particularly for the earlier periods.

4 Norman Munn, *Handbook of Psychological Research on the Rat: An Introduction to Animal Psychology* (Boston, 1950), p. 2.

5 Bob Boakes, *From Darwin to Behaviourism: Psychology and the Minds of Animals* (Cambridge, 1984), p. 143.

6 H. H. Donaldson, *The Rat* (Philadelphia, 1915), p. 1.

7 Logan, '"[A]re Norway rats . . . things?": Diversity Versus Generality in the Use of Albino Rats in Experiments on Development and Sexuality', *Journal of the History of Biology*, XXXIV (2001), p. 289.

8 Chandak Sengoopta, 'Glandular Politics: Experimental Biology, Clinical Medicine, and Homosexual Emancipation in fin-de-siècle Central Europe', *Isis*, LXXXIX (1998), pp. 461–3.

9 Eugen Steinach and Josef Loebel, *Sex and Life* (London, 1940), p. 31.

10 Stewart Richards, 'Anaesthetics, Ethics and Aesthetics: Vivisection in the Late Nineteenth Century British Laboratory', in *The Laboratory Revolution in Medicine*, ed. Andrew Cunningham and Perry Williams (Cambridge, 1992), p. 168.

11 Stephen Kern, *The Culture of Space and Time, 1880–1918* (London, 1983).

12 There is a parallel between rats and the production of laboratory dogs in the 1890s by Pavlov and his co-workers. 'The laboratory dog as technology and organism . . . in the physiological factory [i.e., the laboratory], these dogs were simultaneously technologies, physiological objects of study, and products.' Daniel P. Todes, 'Pavlov's Physiological Factory', *Isis*, LXXXVIII (1997), p. 220.

13 Bonnie T. Clause, 'The Wistar Rat as A Right Choice: Establishing Mammalian Standards and the Ideal of a Standardized Mammal', *Journal of the History of Biology*, XXVI (1993), pp. 306–7.

14 Lindsey, 'Historical Foundations', p. 6.

15 J. Q. Griffith and E. J. Farris (eds), *The Rat in Laboratory Investigation* (Philadelphia, 1942), p. 2.

16 Clause, 'The Wistar Rat as a Right Choice', p. 343.

17 Lynda Birke, 'Who – or What – Are the Rats (and Mice) in the Laboratory?', *Society and Animals*, XI (2003), p. 209.

18 William E. Castle and John C. Phillips, *Piebald Rats and Selection: An Experimental Test of the Effectiveness of Selection and of the Theory of Genetic Purity in Mendelian Crosses* (Washington, DC, 1914), p. 6.

19 Karen Rader, '"The Mouse People": Murine Genetics Work at the Bussey Institution, 1909–1936', *Journal of the History of Biology*, XXXI (1998), p. 339.

20 Michael Lynch, 'Sacrifice and the Transformation of the Animal Body into a Scientific Object: Laboratory Culture and Ritual Practice in the Neurosciences', *Social Studies in Science*, XVIII (1988), pp. 273–4.

21 Henry L. Foster, 'The History of the Commercial Production of Laboratory Rodents', *Laboratory Animal Science*, XXX (1980), p. 794. On a comparable story on the production of laboratory mice, see Karen Rader, 'The Multiple Meanings of Laboratory Animals: Standardising Mice for American Cancer Research, 1910–1950', in *Animals in Human Histories: The Mirror of Nature and Culture*, ed. Mary Henninger-Voss (Rochester, NY, 2002).

22 See, for instance, www.criver.com and also www.harlan.com (accessed July 2004).

23 Fred Quimby, 'Twenty-Five Years of Progress in Laboratory Animal Science', *Laboratory Animals*, XXVIII (1994), p. 163.

24 Norman L. Munn, *Handbook of Psychological Research on the Rat: An Introduction to Animal Psychology* (Boston, MA, 1950), p. 5. Tolman

believed that rats did not simply respond to a stimulus but rather understood its significance and their own behaviour towards it. Moving away from the idea that learning was dependent on rewards and punishments, he thought that they were more like signs indicating the appropriateness and inappropriateness of certain acts. For Tolman the rat is more of an autonomous creature with expectations.

25 Boakes, *Darwin to Behaviourism*, p. 144.

26 John B. Watson, 'Kinaesthetic and Organic Sensations: Their Role in the Reactions of the White Rat in the Maze', *Psychological Review: Psychological Monographs*, 8 (1907), pp. 2–3.

27 Ibid., p. 90.

28 Ibid., p. 99. Later research noted that destruction of the visual cortex in the rat's brain was much more disturbing for maze learning than enucleation of the eyes. Munn, *Handbook of Psychological Research*, p. 225.

29 Boakes, *Darwin to Behaviourism*, p. 147.

30 Robert Nye, *The Legacy of B. F. Skinner: Concepts and Perspectives, Controversies and Misunderstandings* (Pacific Grove, CA, 1992), pp. 13ff.

31 Frederick Wertz, 'Of Rats and Psychologists: A Study of the History and Meaning of Science', *Theory and Psychology*, IV (1994), p. 165.

32 Quoted in K. Shapiro, 'A Rodent for Your Thoughts: The Social Construction of Animal Models', in *Animals in Human Histories*, p. 452.

33 Munn, *Handbook of Psychological Research*, pp. 19–20.

34 L. Shengold, 'The Effects of Overstimulation: Rat People', *International Journal of Psychoanalysis*, XLVIII (1967), p. 413.

35 L. Shengold, 'More about Rats and People', *International Journal of Psychoanalysis*, LII (1971), p. 280.

36 L. Shengold, *Soul Murder: The Effects of Childhood Abuse and Deprivation* (New Haven, 1989), p. 91.

37 S. Freud, *Case Studies II* (Harmondsworth, 1979), p. 47.

38 Ibid., pp. 48–54.

39 Ibid., pp. 93–5. In Viennese dialect *Ratz* can mean little children. The association with marriage is made through the German word, *hieraten*, to marry.

40 Ibid., p. 93.

41 Stanley Weiss notes that at the time in southern Germany and Austria primarily Jewish businessmen were beginning to develop the idea of

buying by instalments. He notes a number of other instances where Ernst appears to be rejecting Jewishness; 'Reflections and Speculations on the Psychoanalysis of the Rat Man', in *Freud and his Patients*, ed. M. Kanzer and J. Glen (New York, 1980), p. 211.

42 S. Freud, 'Original Record of the Case', *Complete Psychological Works: Volume 10* (London, 1955), p. 288.

43 Ibid., p. 311.

44 S. Freud and J. Breuer, 'Studies in Hysteria', *Complete Psychological Works: Volume 2* (London, 1955), p. 289.

45 Freud's Uncle Josef was arrested in 1865 for trying to sell counterfeit money and Freud himself was suspicious of his half-brother Philipp's involvement in counterfeiting. See R. M. Gottlieb, 'Technique and Countertransference in Freud's Analysis of the Rat Man', *Psychoanalytic Quarterly*, LVIII (1989), pp. 51–2. A propos of this Maud Ellmann wrote, 'Just as rats are linked to sexuality and violence so too are they linked to problematic objects of exchange. Indeed, if the rat stands for money we can assume the money to be fake . . . the rat introduces a general economy of waste into the restricted economy of circulation.' J. Burt and M. Ellmann, 'Rat' (unpublished manuscript, 2001), p. 7.

46 S. Freud, *The Origins of Psychoanalysis: Letters to Wilhelm Fliess, Drafts and Notes, 1887–1902* (London, 1954), pp. 107–8

47 Freud, 'Original Record', p. 282.

48 Elizabeth Zetzel (1966) notes that in contrast with the case study there are more than 40 references to a highly ambivalent relationship between mother and son and that the case study underplays Ernst's significant relationships with his mother and sisters; '1965: Additional Notes upon a Case of Obsessional Neurosis: Freud 1909', *International Journal of Psychoanalysis*, XLVII (1966), p. 125.

49 'Pig's Teeth Grown in Rats' Bellies', *New Scientist*, 27 September 2002; 'Infant Rat Heads Grafted onto Adults' Thighs', *New Scientist*, 3 December 2002.

50 S. Talwer et al., 'Behavioural Neuroscience: Rat Navigation Guided by Remote Control', *Nature*, 417 (2002), pp. 37–8.

51 www.fishandchips.uwa.edu.au/project.html (accessed May 2004).

52 Alison Abbott, 'Laboratory Animals: The Renaissance Rat', *Nature*, 428 (2004), pp. 464–6.

53 Kerstin Linbad-Toh, 'Genome Sequencing: Three's Company', *Nature*, 428

(2004), pp. 475–6.

54 Andy Coghlan, 'Rat Genome Reveals Supercharged Evolution', *New Scientist*, 31 March 2004.

55 The population of laboratory animals in the United States in 1978 was put at 90 million, with about 50 million mice and 20 million rats.

56 William Paton, *Man and Mouse: Animals in Medical Research* (2nd edn, Oxford, 1993), p. 3. See the plate on p. 60 for a breakdown of the different areas of medicine worked on using animals since the mid 1890s.

57 Helen Pilcher, 'Rat Genome Unveiled', *Nature*, 1 April 2004. www.nature.com/nsu/040329/040329-11.html (accessed April 2004).

58 Harold B. Hewitt, 'The Uses of Animals in Experimental Cancer Research', in *Animals in Research: New Perspectives in Animal Experimentation*, ed. D. Sperlinger (Chichester, 1981), pp. 168–9.

59 R. Drewett and W. Kani, 'Animal Experimentation in the Behavioural Sciences', in *Animals in Research*, p. 184.

60 Lynch, 'Sacrifice and Transformation', p. 267.

5 PLAGUE AND POLLUTION

1 R. Chandavarkar, 'Plague Panic and Epidemic Politics in India, 1896–1914', in *Epidemics and Ideas: Essays on the Historical Perception of Pestilence*, ed. T. O. Ranger and P. Slack (Cambridge, 1992), p. 203.

2 Quoted in Andrew Cunningham, 'Transforming Plague: The Laboratory and the Identity Of Infectious Disease', in *The Laboratory Revolution in Medicine*, ed. A. Cunningham and P. Williams (Cambridge, 1992), p. 224.

3 G. Twigg, 'The Role of Rodents in Plague Dissemination: A World-Wide Review', *Mammal Review*, VIII (1978), p. 90.

4 Ira Klein, 'Plague, Policy and Popular Unrest in British India', *Modern Asian Studies*, XXII (1988), p. 727.

5 E. H. Hankin, 'On the Epidemiology of Plague', *Journal of Hygiene*, V (1905), pp. 43–4, 73–5.

6 Carol Benedict, *Bubonic Plague in Nineteenth-century China* (Stanford, CA, 1996), p. 167. The plague reservoirs in China are extensive with ten natural plague reservoirs, more than 50 known plague carrying mammals, 40 different insect vectors, and 17 unique strains of plague, p. 2.

7 Peter Pallas, *Novae Species Quadrupedum e Glirium Ordine* (Erlangae,

1778), p. 92.

8 Benedict, *Bubonic Plague*, p. 23. Benedict also quotes another eighteenth-century poet, Shi Daonan: 'Dead rats in the East,/ Dead rats in the West! / As if they were tigers, / Indeed are the people scared. / A few days following the death of the rats, / Men pass away like falling walls.' The rat being taken for a tiger implies that an exaggerated reaction to the rat can be found in other cultures apart from the West. Another observation from Yunnan in 1810 was that in those families that got sick, the rats would jump out and fall dead. Anyone who saw them likewise became ill. See also Samuel Cohn, Jr, *The Black Death Transformed: Disease and Culture in Early Renaissance Europe* (London, 2002), p. 9.

9 Marion Chase, *The Barbary Plague: The Black Death in Victorian San Francisco* (New York, 2003), pp. 151–8.

10 Benedict, *Bubonic Plague in China*, p. 107.

11 Michael W. Dols, *The Black Death in the Middle East* (Princeton, NJ, 1977), p. 39

12 Ibid, p. 89.

13 Quoted in Charles Creighton, *A History of Epidemics in Britain* (2nd edn, London, 1965), vol. I, p. 173.

14 Cohn, *Black Death Transformed*, pp. 132–3.

15 J.-N. Biraben, *Les Hommes et la Peste en France et dans les pays Européens et méditerraneans* (Paris, 1975–6), vol. I, p. 9.

16 Paul Slack, *The Impact of Plague in Tudor and Stuart England* (Oxford, 1990) pp. 218–19.

17 Creighton, *A History of Epidemics*, vol. I, p. 166. This is quoted from a report published in 1852. All subsequent quotes are taken from pp. 166–9.

18 Biraben, *Les Hommes et la Peste*, vol. I, p. 16.

19 For a contemporary consideration of these experiments see 'Reports on Plague Investigations in India', *Journal of Hygiene*, VI (1906), pp. 426–7.

20 Chandavarkar, 'Plague Panic', p. 216. Many scientists and entomologists continued to be dubious. Carlo Tiraboschi's monograph of 1904 on the fleas found on Muridae said the rat-flea hypothesis was inconclusive; 'Les rats, les souris, et leurs parasites cutanés dans leurs rapports avec la propagation de la peste bubonique', *Archives de Parasitologie*, VIII (1904), pp. 174–9.

21 See the rat control policy described in J. A. Thompson, 'On the Epidemiology of Plague', *Journal of Hygiene*, VI (1906), p. 548; also, Bruce

Rosen, 'Australia's Contribution to the Conquest of Plague', *Journal of the Australian Historical Society*, LXIII (1977), pp. 66–7.

22 Klein, 'Plague, Policy', p. 735.

23 G. B. Risse, '"A long pull, a strong pull, and all together": San Francisco and Bubonic Plague, 1907–8', *Bulletin of the History of Medicine*, LXVI (1992), p. 262.

24 Chase, *Barbary Plague*, p. 155.

25 Risse, '"A long pull"', p. 260.

26 Chase, *Barbary Plague*, p. 159.

27 Rupert Blue, 'Anti-Plague Measures in San Francisco, California, USA', *Journal of Hygiene*, IX (1909), pp. 6–7.

28 Chase, *Barbary Plague*, p. 194.

29 John Alexander, *Bubonic Plague in Early Modern Russia: Public Health and Urban Disaster* (Oxford, 2003), pp. 68–9. During a fire in 1753 at the Golovin Palaco, Catherine the Great noticed a huge number of rats and mice descending the staircase en masse 'not even hurrying much', p. 69.

30 A. L. Martin, *Plague?: Jesuit Accounts of Epidemic Disease in the Sixteenth Century* (Kirksville, MI, 1996), p. 204.

31 Slack, *Impact of Plague*, p. 11.

32 Dols, *Black Death in the Middle East*, p. 158. This leads him to conclude that the low rat mortality and high human mortality of the Black Death argues for an infectious pneumonic plague as the most probable disease. Plague was not used as a word for a specific disease until the seventeenth century, nor was the expression the 'Black Death' used in Britain before 1823; see Graham Twigg, *The Black Death: A Biological Reappraisal* (London, 1984), p. 30; J.F.D. Shrewsbury, *A History of Bubonic Plague in the British Isles* (Cambridge, 1970), p. 37.

33 For a useful listing of plagues and their spread prior to the Black Death, see J.-N. Biraben and J. Le Goff, 'The Plague in the Early Middle Ages', in *Biology of Man in History*, ed. R. Forster and O. Ranum (Baltimore, 1975), pp. 48–80.

34 Quoted in Samuel Cohn, Jr, 'The Black Death: End of a Paradigm', *American Historical Review*, CVII (2002), p. 712.

35 G. I. Davys, *Report on the Results of Certain Investigations Regarding Rats in the Punjab* (Calcutta, 1910), pp. 10–11.

36 Twigg, *Black Death*, p. 28.

37 Cohn, 'Black Death', p. 725.

38 Cohn, *Black Death Transformed*, pp. 11–15.

39 Ibid. p. 82.

40 Slack notes that rat populations may gain immunity to plague but the population can become susceptible again within eight years of a major epizootic, 'The Disappearance of Plague: An Alternative View', *English Historical Review*, XXXIV (1981), p. 470.

41 Twigg, *Black Death*, p. 75.

42 G. Karrlson, 'Plague Without Rats: The Case of Fifteenth Century Iceland', *Journal of Medieval History*, XXII (1996), pp. 263–84.

43 M. McCormick, 'Rats, Communication and Plague: Toward an Ecological History', *Journal of Interdisciplinary History*, XXXIV (2003), p. 1.

44 G. Liston, 'The Epidemiology of Plague', *British Medical Journal* (1924), p. 903.

45 Ibid., p. 952.

6 PETS, VERMIN, FOOD

1 'A Fancier is one who by word, action and influence, does all in his or her power to rid this country of the mongrel. The genuine fancier is one who takes a great delight in establishing pedigrees, strains, and pure breeds.' W. L. Langley, 'What is a Fancier? Attractions of the Fancy', *Fur and Feather*, 1 October 1915, p. 226.

2 *Fur and Feather* was founded by J. E. Watmough, a pigeon fancier in Bradford. At first it was known as the *Rabbit Keeper and Show Reporter* before being renamed *Small Pets for Prizes, Pleasure and Profit*. Its first issue as *Fur and Feather* was 1 April 1890, to which was added 'With which is included "Small Pets", a weekly journal devoted to rabbits, cage birds, cats'.

3 M. Tokuda, 'An Eighteenth Century Japanese Guide Book to Mouse Breeding', *Journal of Heredity*, XXVI (1935), pp. 481–4.

4 *Fur and Feather*, 31 October 1901, p. 317.

5 *Fur and Feather*, 28 November 1901, p. 399.

6 On Mary Douglas and the history of the rat fancy see Nick Mays, *The Proper Care of Fancy Rats* (Neptune City, NJ, 1993), pp. 42–74; 'Miss M. D. – Mother of the Rat Fancy', *Pro-Rat-A*, 66 (1991), pp. 6–7; and 'A Rat Odyssey', *Pro-Rat-A*, 121 (2001), pp. 7–9. On Mary Douglas see *Fur and*

Feather, 22 January 1915, p. 43, and Ralph Blake's moving remarks on her death in *Fur and Feather*, 9 December 1921.

7 Tony Jones, 'New Varieties in the Fancy Rat', *Pro-Rat-A*, 112 (1999), p. 8.

8 *Fur and Feather*, 7 March 1895, p. 153; 14 March 1895, p. 168.

9 *Fur and Feather*, 22 June 1917, p. 329.

10 In 1990 it was reported that all the 25 or so varieties then in the rat fancy were from laboratory stock; *Pro-Rat-A*, 60 (1990), p. 8.

11 *Fur and Feather*, 11 December 1914, p. 332.

12 W. R. Boelter, 'On Vermin', *Journal of the Incorporated Society for the Destruction of Vermin*, 1 (1908–9), p. 104. He also notes the German word for vermin, *Ungezeifer*, as 'that which is not fit to serve as an offering to the Deity'.

13 Leonard Mascall, *A Booke of Fishing with Hooke and Line, and of all other instruments thereunto belonging. Another of sundrie Engines and Trappes to take Polcats, Buzards, Rattes, Mice and all other kinds of Vermine and Beasts whatsoever* (London, 1590).

14 W. W., *The Vermin Killer Being a Very Necessary Family Book, containing exact rules and directions for the artificial killing and destroying of all manner of vermin* (London, 1680).

15 Robert Smith, *Universal Directory*, p. 126. This dislike of poisons was common. See, for instance, Colonel George Hanger, *To all Sportsmen and Particularly to Farmers and Gamekeepers* (London, 1814), pp. 86ff.

16 *The Vermin Killer, Being a Compleat and Necessary Family book* (London, n.d.).

17 Mascall, *Sundrie Trappes*, p. 90. W. W. suggests taking the 'scade of wild cowcumbers' and mixing them with colluentida and oat flour for killing rats; *The Vermin Killer*, p. 2.

18 Thomas Swaine, *The Universal Directory for Taking Alive Rats and Mice by a Method hitherto Unattempted* (London, 1783). For an interesting nineteenth-century account of rat-catching, see Ike Matthews, *Full Revelations of a Professional Rat Catcher after 25 years Experience* (Manchester, 1898).

19 Carl Prausnitz, 'The Destruction of Rats on Ships', *Journal of the Incorporated Society for the Destruction of Vermin*, 1 (1908–9), p. 209.

20 Ibid., p. 226.

21 H. E. Annett, 'Virus for the Destruction of Rats and Mice', *British Medical Journal*, 2 (1908), pp. 1524–5.

22 A. P. Meehan, *Rats and Mice: Their Biology and Control* (East Grinstead, 1984), p. 277.

23 Ibid., pp. 141–3.

24 Robert Sullivan, *Rats: Observations on the History and Habitat of the City's Most Unwanted Inhabitants* (New York, 2004), p. 98.

25 James Rodwell, *The Rat: Its History and Destructive Character with Numerous Anecdotes* (London, 1858), pp. 175–6.

26 R. T. Gunther, *Report on Agricultural Damage by Vermin and Birds in the Counties of Norfolk and Oxfordshire in 1916* (Oxford, 1917), p. 14.

27 E. Zuschlag, 'The Rat Law in Denmark: A Review of the First Year's Work', *Journal of the Incorporated Society for the Destruction of Vermin*, I (1908–9), p. 32.

28 M.A.C. Hinton, *Rats and Mice as Enemies of Mankind* (London, 1931), pp. 22–3.

29 See Sir Arthur Griffith-Boscawen's remarks, *Hansard (Commons)*, 27 October 1919, p. 427.

30 Ibid., p. 428.

31 Rodwell, *The Rat*, pp. 130–34.

32 Henry Mayhew, *London Labour and the London Poor* (London, 1861), vol. III, p. 12.

33 T. Y. Canby, 'The Rat: Lapdog of the Devil', *National Geographic*, 152 (1977), p. 69.

34 Vanora Bennett, 'A Plague on All Our Houses', *Prospect*, October 2003.

35 Bourdon de Sigrais, *Histoire des Rats pour servir à l'histoire universelle* (Ratopolis [Paris], 1738), p. 130.

36 Wilkie Collins, *Rambles beyond Railways; or, Notes in Cornwall taken a-foot* (London, 1851), pp. 37–8.

37 Jerry Hopkins, *Strange Foods: An Epicuran's Guide to the Weird and Wonderful* (Boston, MA, 1999).

38 Francis Buckland, *Curiosities of Natural History* (London, 1857), p. 122.

39 Peter Hessler, 'A Rat in my Soup: Looking for the Best Tasting Rodent in Town', *New Yorker*, 24 July 2000.

40 Hopkins, *Strange Foods*, p. 16.

41 André L. Simon, *A Concise Encyclopedia of Gastronomy* (London, 1983), p. 485.

Bibliography

BOOKS

Alderton, David, *Rodents of the World* (London, 1999)

Baker, H. J., J. R. Lindsey and S. H. Weinbroth (eds), *The Laboratory Rat*,
    2 vols (New York, 1979)

Barnett, S. A., *The Rat: A Study in Behaviour* (revd edn, Chicago, 1975)

—, *The Story of Rats* (Crows Nest, NSW, 2001)

Barrett-Hamilton, Gerald, and Martin A. C. Hinton, *A History of British
    Mammals*, part XIX (London, 1916)

Becker, Kurt, *Der Rattenkönig: Eine monographische Studie* (Berlin, 1964)

Benedictow, Ole, *The Black Death, 1346–1355: A Complete History* (Woodbridge,
    2004)

Berchtold, Jacques, *Des Rats et des Ratières: anamorphoses d'un champ
    métaphorique de saint Augustin à Jean Racine* (Geneva, 1992)

Chase, Marion, *The Barbary Plague: The Black Death in Victorian San Francisco*
    (New York, 2003)

Cohn, Jr, Samuel, *The Black Death Transformed: Disease and Culture in Early
    Renaissance Europe* (London, 2002)

Fitzgibbon, Constantine, *The Rat Report*, (London, 1980)

Gessner, Conrad, *Historiae Animalium, Vol. 1* (Cambieriano, 1603)

Golding, Charles, *Rats: The New Plague* (London, 1990)

Grass, Günter, *The Rat* (San Diego, CA, 1987)

Hanney, Peter, *Rodents: Their Lives and Habitats* (Newton Abbott, 1975)

Hart, Martin, *Rats* (London, 1982)

Hogarth, Alfred M., *The Rat: A World Menace* (London, 1929)

Hovell, Mark, *Rats and How to Destroy Them* (London, 1924)

Kotzwinkle, W., *Doctor Rat* (London, 1984)

Krüger, Sabine, *Die Figur der Ratte in literarischen Texten: Eine Motivstudie*

(Frankfurt am Main, 1989)

Mahoney, Patrick, *Freud and the Rat Man* (New Haven, 1986)

Mascall, Leonard, *A Booke of Fishing with Hooke and Line, and of all other instruments thereunto belonging: Another of sundrie Engines and Trappes to take Polcats, Buzards, Rattes, Mice and all other kinds of Vermine and Beasts whatsoever* (London, 1590)

Matthews, Ike, *Full Revelations of a Professional Rat Catcher after 25 Years Experience* (Manchester, 1898)

Mays, Nick, *The Proper Care of Fancy Rats* (Neptune City, NJ, 1993)

Meehan, A. P., *Rats and Mice: Their Biology and Control* (East Grinstead, 1984)

Munn, Norman, *Handbook of Psychological Research on the Rat: An Introduction to Animal Psychology* (Boston, MA, 1950)

O'Brien, Robert, *Mrs Frisby and the Rats of NIMH* (Harmondsworth, 1982)

Olds, R. J., and J. R. Olds, *A Colour Atlas of the Rat: Dissection Guide* (London, 1991)

Rader, Karen, *Making Mice: Standardising Animals for American Biomedical Research* (Princeton, NJ, 2004)

Rodwell, James, *The Rat: Its History and Destructive Character with Numerous Anecdotes* (London, 1858)

Rosevear, D. R., *The Rodents of West Africa* (London, 1969)

Shengold, Leonard, *Soul Murder: The Effects of Childhood Abuse and Deprivation* (New Haven, 1989)

Shrewsbury, J.F.D., *A History of Bubonic Plague in the British Isles* (Cambridge, 1970)

Sigrais, C. G. Bourdon de, *Histoire des Rats* (Ratopolis [Paris], 1738)

Smith, Robert, *The Universal Directory for Taking Alive and Destroying Rats and All Other Kinds of Four-footed and Winged Vermin* (London, 1768)

Sullivan, Robert, *Rats: Observations on the History and Habitat of the City's Most Unwanted Inhabitants* (New York, 2004)

Swaine, Thomas, *The Universal Directory for taking alive rats and mice by a method hitherto unattempted* (London, 1783)

Sykes Davis, Hugh, *The Papers of Andrew Melmoth* (London, 1960)

Thompson, Silvanus, *The Pied Piper of Hamelin* (London, 1905)

Topsell, Edward, *The Historie of the Four-footed Beasts* (London, 1607)

Twigg, Graham, *The Brown Rat* (Newton Abbott, 1975)

—, *The Black Death: A Biological Reappraisal* (London, 1984)

West, Paul, *Rat Man of Paris* (London, 1988)

Wiesner, B. P., and N. M. Sheard, *Maternal Behaviour in the Rat* (Edinburgh, 1933)

Zaniewski, Andrzej, *Rat* (New York, 1994)

Zinsser, Hans, *Rats, Lice and History* (Harmondsworth, 2000)

JOURNALS

Pro-Rat-A: The National Fancy Rat Society Journal (UK)

Rat News Letter (Medical Research Council) (UK)

The Rat Report (USA)

Associations and Websites

www.worldratday.com
   The website for events relating to World Rat Day

www.nfrs.org
   The British National Fancy Rat Society website

www.ratfanclub.org
   The Rat Fan Club has useful links, especially to other societies and groups
   in the USA

Acknowledgements

I would like to thank Kevin Jackson, Erica Fudge, Debora Greger, Rebecca Stott, Ken Shapiro, Drake Stutesman, John Burton, Garry Marvin, Rita Copeland, Eleanor Burt, Tabitha Buck, Lynda Birke, Nick Mays, Fay Hogben, Guy Ben-Ary, Tim Mackrell, Sara Olson, Remo Campopiano, Michael Leaman and Rick Cicciarelli. I am very indebted to Harry Gilonis for work on the images. Finally, I have the biggest debt to Nicky Zeeman for translating Gessner and Peter Pallas for me as well as enduring the enthusiasms and depressions that come from writing about rats.

I have also received the support of the British Academy for *Rat*, for which I am extremely grateful.

I would like to point out to avid readers that the inclusion of any pictures of rats that are really mice is entirely intentional.

This book is for my parents and Professor B for teaching me the biggest lesson of all.

Photo Acknowledgements

The author and publishers wish to express their thanks to the below sources of illustrative material and/or permission to reproduce it. (Some sources uncredited in the captions for reasons of brevity are also given below.)

© ARS, New York and DACS, London, 2005 p. 14 (foot); courtesy of the artist: pp. 59 (Remo Campopiano), 77 (Manon Cleary); The Ashmolean Museum of Art and Archaeology, Oxford: p. 70; British Library, London: pp. 11 (top), 17, 53, 64 (top), 75; © David Falconer/courtesy of Stuart Shave, Modern Art, London: p. 87; photo Michael Freeman p. 146; Getty Images: pp. 98, 100, 111; Guildhall Library, London: p. 73; courtesy Fay Hogben: p. 131; photo Library of Congress, Washington, DC (Chadbourne collection of Japanese prints; gift of Mrs E. Crane Chadbourne; LC-USZC4-10397): p. 35; photo courtesy of Tim Mackrell: p.67; Mary Evans Picture Library: pp. 14 (top), 16, 58 (top right), 68, 74, 99 (foot); photos courtesy of Nick Mays: pp. 122 (© Cambridge University Press), 132, 133; National Geographic: pp. 57 (foot), 58 (left and lower right), 123; Natural History Museum, London: p.22; photo Department of Psychology, Nebraska Wesleyan University, Lincoln: p. 135; Pierpont Morgan Library, New York: p. 38 top left (from the *Dioscorides Codex*, Cod. N.Y. Morgan M652, fol. 208v); photo Rex Features: p.101 (449013 AA); photo Rex Features/Boyer/Roger-Viollet: p. 19 (BOY-8164; 601-13); photos Roger-Viollet/Rex Features: pp. 6 (RVB-09831; 10841-1), 9 (RV-59549; 2883-12), 88 (RV-357463B; 263-13), 147 (RV-8733-8), 148 (RV-8733-9); photos Science Photo Library, London: pp. 96, 99 (top); State Records, New South Wales, Australia: p. 120; photo Drake Stutesman: p. 76; Symbiotica, University of Western Australia: p. 112; Topkapi Sarayi Library, Istanbul: p. 10 (from the *Warqa wa Gulshāh*, Ms Haz 841); photos University Library, Cambridge: pp. 11 (foot), 14 (foot), 18, 29, 32, 38 (foot), 39, 62–63, 72 (foot), 79,

Index